Nurturing Your Newborn
Young Parents' Guide to Baby's First Month

Jeanne Warren Lindsay, MA, CFCS
and Jean Brunelli, PHN, MA

Morning
Glory
Press

Buena Park, California

Nurturing Your Newborn
is part of a six-book series. Other titles are:

*Your Pregnancy and Newborn Journey:
A Guide for Pregnant Teens*

*Your Baby's First Year:
A Guide for Teenage Parents*

*The Challenge of Toddlers:
For Teen Parents — Parenting Your Child from One to Three*

*Discipline from Birth to Three: How Teen Parens Can Prevent
and Deal with Discipline Problems with Babies and Toddlers*

Teen Dads: Rights, Responsibilities and Joys

Library of Congress Cataloging-in-Publication Data
Lindsay, Jeanne Warren.
    Nurturing your newborn : young parents' guide to baby's
first month / by Jeanne Warren Lindsay and Jean Brunelli.
    p.   cm.
    Includes bibliographical references (p.).
    ISBN 1-932538-20-8
    1. Infants (Newborn) --Care Juvenile literature. 2. Teen-
age mothers Juvenile literature. 3. Mother and infant Juve-
nile literature. I. Brunelli, Jean, 1932- . II. Title.
HQ774.L55 1999
649'. 122--dc21   99-25877
                                                                    CIP

MORNING GLORY PRESS, INC.
6595 San Haroldo Way   Buena Park, CA 90620-3748
714/828-1998   1/888-612-8254
http://www.morninggglorypress.com
Printed and bound in the United States of America

Contents

Foreword

The most amazing thing happens when a baby is born. This very small someone who once was hiding out of sight makes his squalling entrance into the world and nothing is ever again as it was before! There are feedings, and diapers to change, baths to give, and lots of cuddling to do. The weight of responsibility for your baby and the promise of the incredible potential for what she might become fills you up and helps you through the most exciting, wonderful, exhausting and scary undertaking that you have ever experienced. Welcome to the "hood," Parenthood, that is!

In your hands is a wonderful tool. Jeanne Lindsay and Jean Brunelli wrote this guidebook for you. Think of it as a map to steer you through the early weeks as you care for your baby. Through their years of experience and ongoing relationship with young parents, Jeanne and Jean have become experts in communicating with new parents. You'll find this small book extremely valuable as you discover the unique qualities of your baby. After all, no two babies are the same — but they all have similarities. Each has an individual personality, and each needs to be totally loved.

I remember when I was a first-time mother. I was so scared, yet I wanted to prove to the world (and especially to my own mother) that I was perfectly capable of being a loving mother, and that I could be the best parent ever. I wanted only the best for my son, but I had so many questions that I didn't know where to begin. How I wish I had a book such as this one to help me!

Ms. Lindsay was my teacher then, and I knew she believed in me, as I gained confidence in my ability to parent, and I practiced becoming a great mother. I wanted to know *everything,* and I worried if I wasn't doing all of it "just right." Thank goodness my son had never had a mother before, so he couldn't compare me to anyone else! I made lots of mistakes, as we learned about each other. You will also make mistakes — but you will also learn as I did.

That was nearly 25 years ago. It appears that my son survived those early weeks just fine, and I did, too. He got all of the very best I had to offer — my two breasts to nurse him, my two arms to hold him, and my whole heart to love him. I got better at being his mother, and, of course, he was perfect at being a baby!

Your baby is lucky to have you as his/her parent, because you are interested in knowing more. This book is a great place to start. Learn all you can about your baby. Read as much as possible, watch others whom you consider to be "good parents" as they take care of and interact with their children, ask loads of questions, and don't be too shy to consult with those who are the experts. And, after you've done all these things, if the information doesn't seem to make sense, or match what you know is right, trust yourself and follow your heart. After all, you'll be your child's parent for many years, and you love your baby the most of all!

Teresa McFarland, R.N.

To the young parents whose comments
about loving and caring for their infants
add so much to this book.

Acknowledgments

*We are especially grateful to the young people quoted in
Nurturing Your Newborn. Some of the quotes also appear in Your
Pregnancy and Newborn Journey and Your Baby's First Year, and
these young people are acknowledged there.*

*Those interviewed especially for Nurturing Your Newborn
include Sophia Campbell, Karina Lopez, Monica Acosta, Maria
Perez, Mia Tamargo, Philip Chapman, Mike Hernandez, Tiana
Garcia, Carrie Martinez, Jasmine Thurman, and LaTasha B.
Quotes are used with assumed names.*

*We appreciate David Crawford's photos of his students at
William Daylor High School, Sacramento, California, as well as
photos from Carole Blum. Jan Oehrke, lactation consultant, and
Teresa McFarland shared their expertise, especially in chapter 2.
We thank them.*

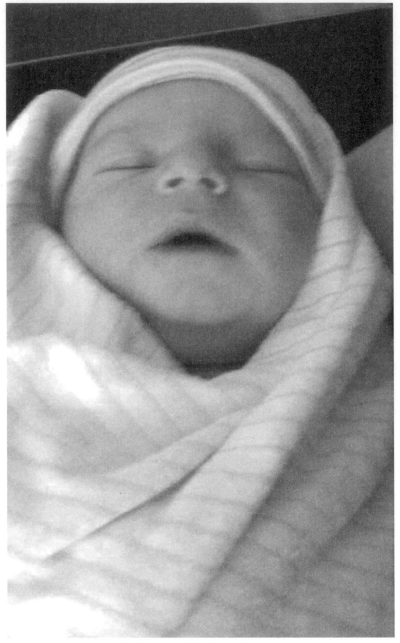

Your baby is totally dependent on you.

1

Coming Home with Your Baby

- A Blur
  of Tiredness

- Bonding with
  Your Baby

- Do You
  Sometimes
  Feel Sad?

- Involving Dad

- You May Get
  Frustrated

- Doing Something
  for *You*

When I came home I just wanted to go to sleep. My room was a mess but I didn't care. My mom helped me with the baby.

Sumaire, 17 - Cassidy, 6 weeks

Take naps when your baby does. It helps a lot. I rarely took naps because I had to wash clothes, clean house, all that stuff. But when I did, it made me feel better.

Zaria, 16 - Devyn, 3 months

Once he was cleaned up and I finally got to hold him, I couldn't take my eyes off him. He was beautiful.

Marina, 17 - Rudi, 1 week

A Blur of Tiredness

Those first weeks with your new baby may seem like a blur, a time of constant activity and tiredness. Your baby may need to be fed every couple of hours. She may be awake much of the night, then sleep most of the day.

Sometimes I'm like a zombie when he wakes up at night. I change his diaper, feed him. Sometimes I think, "Can't you just sleep?" but I can't think that way, get angry. I just get over it.

Marina

You'll probably be terribly tired when you get home from the hospital. You're tired because you worked hard during labor. You're tired from interrupting your sleep by feeding your baby whenever she's hungry. In addition to all this, you can blame your hormones.

Those hormone changes that occurred during pregnancy are now changing back to your non-pregnant state. Even that is tiring.

Did you have an episiotomy (small cut made to enlarge the vaginal opening)? If so, your stitches are likely to hurt the first few days. Moms who have a C-section (cesarean delivery) will recover from childbirth more slowly than those who delivered vaginally.

Once my body heals completely, it will be a lot easier. I had two stitches, and it hurts to sit down, to use the bathroom. Everything takes so long.

Marina

You'll be having some bleeding for about two weeks. Occasionally a blood clot will come out, too. These are from the area where the placenta separated from the uterus. If, after a few days, the bleeding is still bright red, call your healthcare provider.

Use sanitary pads rather than tampons to care for the bleeding after delivery. The tissue is so soft a tampon could go up high in your vagina; you'd have a problem getting it out. An infection could then develop, and you could get quite sick.

Especially if you're breastfeeding, it's a good idea to continue taking your prenatal vitamins. This will help you avoid anemia and speed your recovery.

Your temperature might change as your hormones change gears. Always check your temperature if you feel sick. You might have an infection and need to call your healthcare provider.

Four to six weeks after your baby is born you need to see your healthcare provider. Be *sure* to keep this appointment. She will check your health and make sure you're recovering well from pregnancy and delivery. If you haven't already talked with her about birth control, this is a good time to do so.

> *We'd like another baby once we have our own place and our jobs, really settled — maybe in a couple of years. I'll use the patch.*
>
> Allegra, 17 - Navaeh, 6 weeks

If you don't want another baby right away, ask her about the patch, Depo-Provera, birth control pills, and other methods. Then decide which will work best for you.

Bonding with Your Baby

> *I talk to her and I cuddle her. She likes that. She stares at me until I talk to her, and then she will smile. I just want to see her smile. That makes me happy.*
>
> Allegra

As you bond with your baby, you'll feel much like you're falling in love. You'll probably feel this surge of love, this bonding. However, sometimes a mom doesn't feel as strong a bond with her newborn as other moms seem to have. If her life isn't going as well as she'd like, it may be harder for her to develop a strong bond with her baby.

What encourages this falling-in-love feeling? Feed your baby, hold him, brag about him to your friends, show him off to other people. You'll probably get these intense feelings of love.

At first, when you talk, smile, and interact with your baby, he may not seem to pay much attention to you. Nevertheless, it's very important that you talk with him from the day he's born. As you talk, he learns to trust you and the rest of his world. Talking with him now will also help him work toward developing language skills later.

Important: Always place your baby on her back when you lay her down to sleep. Babies who sleep on their backs are much less likely to develop SIDS (Sudden Infant Death Syndrome).

Do You Sometimes Feel Sad?

Frustrations? The first night when she didn't sleep, and when she had colic. Sometimes at night she gets real fussy and wants me to rock her to sleep. When I get frustrated, I tell my boyfriend to take her. Or I try to calm down because I know it won't work if I'm frustrated.

                                                                    Allegra

Most young moms think, in spite of their tiredness, that they *should* be completely delighted with this new baby. Yet a lot of mothers are unhappy at least part of the time during this first week or two. If this happens to you, know that you're not alone.

At least half, perhaps 80 percent, of mothers get these

after-baby blues. You may be sad as you think about how much work a baby takes and how tied down you are with this tiny helpless child. But, if you're feeling blue, you also have a physical reason. Your body is adjusting to being non-pregnant. Your hormones are working hard to get over those nine months of pregnancy. So you may feel pretty mixed up at times.

> *The first night was really hard. Navaeh didn't sleep at all, not even for ten minutes. I was really frustrated. Then my mother-in-law came in and helped me out. In the morning she took Navaeh so me and my boyfriend could sleep.*
>
> Allegra

If you can get some help with baby care, your after-baby blues may not be so strong. Most important is to find some time somehow to do things you want to do for yourself. Can you get away from the house for a couple of hours?

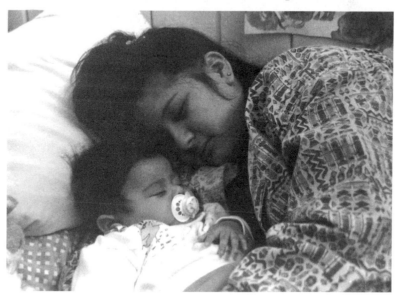

You need to sleep while baby sleeps.

Perhaps go to the mall or a movie? You'll feel much better if you do.

Even taking baby outside for a little while will help. A change of scenery may make you both feel better.

It's important to share your feelings with someone. When you keep unhappy feelings bottled up inside, you're likely to feel worse.

Make a point of finding help when you need it. Know that you are entitled to finish school, and you may be eligible for food stamps and financial aid.

Learn all you can about opportunities for job training, daycare services, helpful church programs, social programs, and other support possibilities in your area. Your teacher, healthcare provider, or social worker should have helpful information. Give them a call.

Know that you aren't weird if, even as you look at your beautiful new baby, you feel sad. You are normal, and you'll likely feel better soon.

However, if you feel depressed for more than a couple of weeks, your situation could be more serious. If so, you need to check with your healthcare provider about other kinds of help.

Involving Dad

If you're with your baby's father, whether or not you're married and/or living together, encourage him to be involved in baby care. When he is, everyone wins. You'll have some of the help you need with baby. The more dad does with baby, the faster he'll bond with his child. Your baby wins by having two loving parents.

Be careful that you, the baby's mom, don't suggest through words or actions that only you know what to do when baby cries. If you criticize your husband/boyfriend, he may soon decide that caring for baby is, indeed, your job, not his to share. He may think he's not needed, and that he's being left out of this whole parenting business.

Perhaps he hasn't had much experience with tiny infants. If he seems afraid of doing the wrong thing, show him how to diaper, feed, and rock baby. With practice, he may feel better about the whole situation.

A peaceful home is important to a baby. If you and your partner or other members of your family are upset with each other, baby will sense the stress. Jeanne, 16, mother of two-month-old Eric, explained:

Your home life has a lot to do with a child. If I'm tense, he is, too. If a lot of yelling goes on, it bothers the baby. Sometimes Mike and I fight, but we don't in front of Eric. It's bad to do that because he can feel the tension, and it's not good for him.

You would think a two-month-old baby wouldn't know, but they do. If they hear you fighting, it's bad.

You May Get Frustrated

Sometimes Jesse was very fussy those first weeks. God, sometimes I wish I could just get up and leave because I'm so tired of not being able to do whatever I want.

I'm trying not to have these feelings, but I can't help it. I just wonder, are they wrong? Am I a horrible mother for thinking like that? I hope not.

Frederica, 16 - Jesse, 5 months

Of course Frederica is not a bad mother for having these very real feelings. Most of us get more tense as the baby cries harder. The problem then is that the baby feels the parent's tenseness and is even more upset.

Acting on one's frustration by hurting the baby is certainly wrong. Some parents resort to child abuse. Perhaps you've heard a parent angrily say to a crying child, "If you don't quit that crying, you're getting a spanking." That's not very sensible, is it? It doesn't help the parent, and it certainly doesn't make the child feel better.

Sometimes a parent may feel like shaking baby. Shaking is absolutely the wrong thing to do. Shaking can damage a baby's brain. See that no one *ever* shakes your baby.

When you're upset because of baby's crying, you'll help your baby if you can possibly relax. Try thinking about something you really like doing or fantasizing about your favorite place. Your baby may relax as you do.

> *When Devyn is crying and crying and crying, I get*
> *so mad. Then I start singing to him and everything is*
> *fine after that. Singing helps with the frustrations.*
>
> Zaria, 16 - Devyn, 3 months

Sometimes your baby will cry because she doesn't feel well. Is she feverish? See chapter 5 for more about caring for baby when she's not feeling well.

If you're bottle-feeding and your baby cries a lot, perhaps her formula isn't right for her. Talk with your health professional. Perhaps she will suggest a different formula.

As you get to know your baby, you'll find other ways to help her be more comfortable.

Doing Something for *You*

All mothers (and fathers) need to learn ways of dealing with this stress. Sometimes it means someone else giving you a break. It may mean leaving the housework and going to visit a friend for a change of pace. Sometimes it may mean calling a hotline. Every mother is going to have these feelings at least occasionally.

What can a mom do when she gets tense and frustrated and there's no one else to take care of her baby? It might be better to put her baby in his crib where she knows he's safe, then walk away for a few minutes. Sometimes this is better for the baby than mom trying to cope with more than she can handle right then. (Of course you'll *never* leave your baby alone in an empty house or apartment.)

Much as you love your baby, you're likely to get upset with him occasionally. Don't feel guilty. Sometimes a mom knows she needs to get away, but she feels too guilty to do anything about it. But sometimes it's necessary, especially for a single parent who can't poke the other parent in the back and say, "It's your turn now."

If you're living alone, can you ask your next-door neighbor for help occasionally? Plan a way to get away when you know you need to.

Exercising can help ease tension. Doing the prenatal exercises you learned during pregnancy won't hurt you or your stitches. Neither will the relaxation techniques you practiced during pregnancy. You don't want to do more vigorous exercise until your bleeding has stopped. Stop exercising and rest if you start feeling light-headed.

If your baby needs to be held and you have work to do, get a sturdy sling carrier. Then you can carry her on your chest. She can be close to you even when you're using your hands for other activities.

When your baby is riding in the car, of course, she *must* be in a sturdy car seat in the back facing the rear of the car. Being in your arms while she's riding is *not* safe for her.

Some parents find the first month with baby is almost easy because their baby sleeps most of the time. Others say those first weeks are the most difficult. Whichever way you feel, love your baby, give her attention when she needs it, and remember to look after yourself, too. After all, *you are your baby's most important person!*

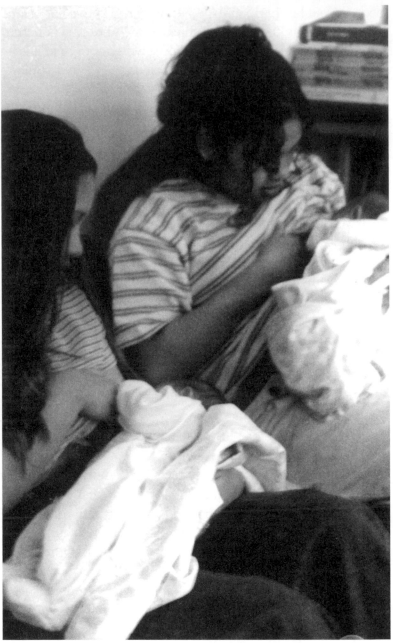

Breastfeeding is best for both baby and mom.

2

Feeding and Loving
Your Newborn

*Breastfeeding is really handy.
When I go places, I pump because
I almost always use breast milk. I
tried formula once, but Patty spit
it up.*

*I'm breastfeeding because they
say it's good for the baby. But it's
also handy and saves money. You
don't have to get up and heat the
bottle. That's when I especially
like it.*

Beth, 18 - Patty, 3 weeks

*I wanted to give her the best start.
I didn't have a house or a back
yard for her to play in, but I could
breastfeed her. She deserved the
best start she could have.*

Zandra, 16 - Dakota, 1 month

Why Some Moms Choose Breastfeeding

I feel bonded to Jenilee. I think it's because I breastfeed her. When she cries, I'm the one that gets her, and I feed her and she's better. She stares up at me like she already loves me.

Lacey, 16 - Jenilee, 1 month

A big decision you've probably made already is whether to breastfeed or bottle-feed your baby. If you've decided to breastfeed, at least for a little while, these may be your reasons:

• You know this is best for your baby
• Baby is less likely to get sick if you breastfeed.
• Breastfeeding is less expensive than buying formula.
• Breastfeeding, once baby and mom have gotten a good start, is easier for mom. (No bottles to sterilize, no formula to mix, *and* you don't have to heat the bottle!)

A young mom told me she quit trying to breastfeed while she was in the hosital because her breasts were not producing "milk." At least, it didn't look like milk to her.

I wish she had known about colostrum, the "milk" your breasts produce the first few days after delivery. This is a "super" milk, low in volume and high in nutrition. It's a yellowish substance, which contains water, some sugar, minerals, and many important antibodies. Colostrum is high in fat and calories, so the small quantity available for baby is fine. He does *not* need a bottle of formula!

Even if you breastfeed your baby only for a few days, you'll give him a good start because colostrum gives him some protection against illness.

If your breasts are small, don't worry. The amount of milk you make depends on how often your baby nurses. If your nipples are flat or inverted, getting baby latched on may be difficult. Once baby is latched on, it'll be okay. If you have difficulty with latching on because of inverted nipples, apply something cold, such as an ice cube or cold washcloth first. This should help.

You may have heard that breastfeeding your baby will make your breasts sag. No, this shouldn't happen, although your breasts become larger during pregnancy. Wearing a good supportive bra during pregnancy and while you're breastfeeding helps prevent sagging.

If baby's dad is around, tell him he shouldn't feel left out when you breastfeed. Explain that you're breastfeeding so baby will have the best possible start in life. Dad can help with all the other baby care tasks. He can bathe baby, change her diapers, and play with her. Remind him how much babies need love and cuddling when they're *not* nursing.

Breastfed Babies May Be Healthier

Breastfeeding is much easier compared to Mom's friend who had a baby about the time I had Stevie. She's bottle-feeding him. He's had three colds already, and Stevie's had none. Her baby cries a lot, too.

Alison, 18 - Stevie, 2 months

Did you know that breastfed babies tend to be healthier during their first year than their bottle-fed friends? A breastfed baby is less likely to catch a cold. That's a real bonus. Just think how hard it is for a tiny baby who can't breathe easily because he can't blow his nose. That's difficult for both mom and baby.

Breastfeeding is not a guarantee against colds that first year. And some bottle-fed babies may not catch a cold in those early months. All we know is that breastfed babies are *less likely* to get sick than are their bottle-fed friends. They are less likely to develop allergies, earaches, diarrhea,

constipation, or tooth decay. Breastfeeding also helps your
baby's brain grow.

If you catch cold or get the flu, should you continue
breastfeeding your baby? *Yes!* If he does get sick, the
antibodies in your breast milk will help him recover faster.

While you were pregnant, perhaps you didn't make a
firm decision about breast- or bottle-feeding. That's cer-
tainly okay. If you breastfeed your baby for just a few days,
he'll get that wonderful colostrum. If you decide
breastfeeding isn't for you, then you can switch to bottles.

Perhaps you've decided you prefer to bottle-feed your
baby. That's okay. Above all, don't feel guilty. You cer-
tainly can be a "good" mother, no matter which feeding
method you choose.

In a few cases, it's actually best for mom to bottle-feed.
If she smokes heavily, takes drugs, or is infected with the
HIV virus, which causes AIDS, she should not breastfeed.
Drugs and nicotine are carried through the milk to the baby.
Perhaps you only take a prescription drug. Nevertheless,
you need to ask your healthcare provider if the drug would
affect breastfeeding.

Don't even take over-the-counter medications when
you're breastfeeding. They might affect your milk and
your baby.

Techniques for Beginning Breastfeeding

Hold baby on his side facing you when you start to nurse
him. His tummy will face yours. To get him started, touch
his lower lip with your finger or nipple. He has a rooting
reflex action ready to go when he's born. When you touch
his lip, his mouth will open. As it opens, bring him to your
nipple. Be sure his bottom lip curls out. If it doesn't, pull
his chin down gently.

Latching on: The term used for the baby
getting your nipple into his mouth.

Most of the areola (dark area around your nipple) should
be in his mouth when he sucks. That's where the milk
pools. Your nipples should not get sore if he latches on
properly.

> *Monday I had a breastfeeding doctor's appoint-*
> *ment. There were four of us there with our babies, and*
> *she had us demonstrate breastfeeding. I thought he*
> *was latching on, and it wasn't hurting much, but he*
> *was doing it wrong. She had him open his mouth real*
> *wide, and then she shoved the nipple way in. It felt*
> *totally different. It suddenly didn't hurt at all.*
>
> Marina, 17 - Rudi, 1 week

If baby sucked only on the end of your nipple, it would
hurt you. He wouldn't get as much milk either. You can
avoid this pain by being sure baby's mouth opens wide onto
the areola. Nurse for a few minutes on each side at each
feeding session the first day or two. After that, nurse for as
long as baby wants to nurse.

You don't need to hide in your bedroom while you
breastfeed. Your baby wants to eat when she's hungry. It's
much harder for her to wait awhile than it would be for us.
Just throw a blanket over your baby, and you should be
able to breastfeed almost anywhere.

> *One time we were at Mike's baseball game, and I*
> *went to the car to feed Eric. When Mike and his*
> *friends came back, I had him all covered up with a*
> *blanket while I nursed him. They said, "Sh-h, he's*
> *asleep." I smiled and nodded.*
>
> Jeanne, 16 - Eric, 2 months

Let Baby Set Mealtime

Tiny babies need to be fed when they're hungry. They can't tell time for a few years yet, so their hunger pains are *not* clock directed. They're simply hungry when they're hungry. And they *don't* cry to exercise their lungs! (Simply breathing gives those lungs plenty of exercise.)

During the first couple of months, most of your baby's crying is probably due to hunger. Offer her your breast or a bottle first. If she doesn't want food, naturally you don't try to force her to eat. You look for other reasons for her crying, like wet or dirty diapers. But first you offer breast or formula.

You'll be feeding your baby at least 8-12 times each 24 hours during the first month or so. You may even need to wake him occasionally for feeding during the first couple of weeks. Remember, if he eats every 2-21/2 hours during the day, he's likely to sleep for longer periods at night.

If you offer the left breast first at one feeding, start with the right one the next time so that baby will empty each one completely. This is important so that your breasts will "know" to produce more milk on both sides. Hint: Attach a diaper pin to your bra strap on the side baby finishes nursing. You'll remember to start on that side next time.

Feed your baby at the first sign of hunger, such as increased activity, mouthing, or rooting. Waiting until she's crying is not necessary, and could give baby more difficulty with breastfeeding.

The more often you nurse your baby, the more milk your breasts will produce. As we said before, proper latch-on will help prevent sore nipples.

If your nipples get sore, keep them dry and expose them to air. Rub a little breast milk into each nipple after you finish feeding your baby. Avoid creams and lanolin. For persistent soreness, get help.

Your breasts will feel heavy and full during the first week after you deliver. This will happen whether you're breastfeeding or bottle-feeding your baby. Breastfeed your baby, and your breasts will feel more comfortable in a day or two. Try putting a warm washcloth on your breasts and massaging them before you start nursing. Massaging during feeding also helps.

It was hard for him to latch on when my breasts were engorged. Once I got home he was waking up every hour to 1 1/2 hours to eat, and that was hard. I almost quit, but I didn't. It's frustrating at first, but if you keep at it, it's better for him. He learned real quick how to latch on.

Tiana, 15 - Francisco, 3 months

If your breast is very full or especially hard, baby may find it difficult to latch on. It will help if you hand express or pump a little milk first. This may soften the areola so

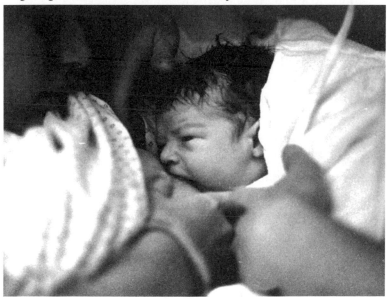

Breastfeeding increases the bond between mom and baby.

baby can latch on more easily. Any milk you express can be frozen for later use.

An ice pack under your armpits may help if your breasts are still sore after he nurses. That's because the breast tissue starts there. Or try a warm shower and breast massage. Some people suggest that putting green cabbage leaves on your sore breasts will give relief much as ice does.

You may find that milk leaks from your breasts between feedings. If so, you can protect your clothes with purchased disposable or cloth pads. Pads you can make yourself are just as effective. Cut a cloth diaper into small pieces about three inches square. Sew several layers together, then put in your bra as needed. They're easily washed.

As soon as baby stops nursing at one breast, burp him. Easiest way is to hold him up to your shoulder and rub his back gently. Breastfed babies tend to burp less than babies fed with a bottle. This is because they don't usually swallow as much air as bottle-fed babies.

For a good start with breastfeeding, it's wise not to give the baby a bottle at least during the first month. This gives your breasts and your baby a chance to get well started with breastfeeding.

After the first six weeks, you may decide to give your baby a bottle occasionally. There may be an emergency sometime when you can't be there. This will also give grandma and dad a chance to feed the baby.

Remember, your breasts create more milk only if stimulated by baby's nursing — or if you express milk (squeeze out) by hand or with a breast pump.

Get Help When You Need It

The first three days in the hospital she wouldn't latch on, and when she did, she would just take my nipple and that hurt real bad. Then once I got home she got the hang of it and so did I. It worked really good then.

Allegra, 17 - Navaeh, 6 weeks

If your baby doesn't appear willing to nurse at first, take off her clothes except for her diaper. Then hold her close. Lots of skin-to-skin contact helps a baby figure out what she needs to do. Cuddle her and try to express a little milk into her mouth. If she still doesn't suck, don't think giving her a bottle is the solution. That would only confuse her.

Or someone may suggest that you don't have enough milk for your baby and that you should switch to formula. *Know that almost all new moms can breastfeed successfully.* If it doesn't seem to be working for you and your baby, call your healthcare provider and ask for lactation help. Don't ask if you should quit breastfeeding.

Some WIC offices have breastfeeding peer support counselors. You should also be able to get help with breastfeeding from maternity ward nurses, or lactation specialists. Possibly a breastfeeding specialist in your healthcare provider's office can also help you.

The La Leche League chapter in your community (if there is one) is another good source for help with breastfeeding. La Leche League is an organization of breastfeeding mothers. A local group will usually have a series of several meetings dealing with the how-to of breastfeeding. Members are available to help each other find answers to questions or problems with breastfeeding.

You may find La Leche League in your local telephone directory. Or you could call your local hospital labor and delivery unit for information about the local chapter of LLL. Then call the League to learn of meetings of possible interest to you. If you have problems with breastfeeding, you can usually get help by calling their number.

How Much Is Enough?

If you're breastfeeding, your baby will "tell" you if she's getting enough milk. She's getting plenty if:

• She has at least six to eight wet diapers each day and several soft mustard-color BMs after one week of age.

• She seems satisfied for at least one or two hours after each feeding.

Your baby may seem especially hungry when he's about two weeks old, again at six weeks, and at three months. He needs more food at these times, and you may think you don't have enough milk for him. You're probably right.

This is *not* the time to bring on the bottles, however. The solution is simply to nurse the baby more often. This lets your breasts know to make more milk.

Your baby controls your supply of milk. Usually it takes about two days of nursing more often to make more milk. Then she will level out to nursing less often again. She'll also be more content.

Your breastfed baby doesn't need additional water or any other food for the first four to six months, according to the American Academy of Pediatrics.

Taking Care of You

Paula only cries when she's hungry, cold or lonely. Last night she was waking up every 15 minutes. She wanted me to hold her until she went to sleep.

Breastfeeding is working fine. I didn't have much soreness, only the second day when my milk came in. I gave her a little water once, but she doesn't seem to need that since she's breastfeeding.

Deanna, 15 - Paula, 3 weeks

When you're caring for a baby, you especially need to take good care of yourself. While you're breastfeeding, it's extra important that you eat the nutritious foods you needed while you were pregnant.

You need about 500 extra calories each day. A sandwich and two extra glasses of milk in addition to your "regular" nutritious diet should be enough.

Drink enough liquids, too. You need 8 to 12 glasses daily of water, milk, fruit juices, etc., so drink whenever you get thirsty. "Liquids" is the key word. You don't have to drink milk to make breast milk. If you like it or can drink it, include it as part of your liquids. If not, get your calcium from other sources such as green leafy vegetables and calcium-fortified orange juice.

It's best for the baby if you can limit your drinking of coffee, tea, and soft drinks to two cups each day. Avoid caffeinated beverages. Choose decaf versions instead.

When you nurse your baby, sit (or lie) in a comfortable place. Put your feet up and enjoy your baby. Drink one of those many glasses of liquid you need each day.

Learn to relax while you're feeding baby. Your milk flows more easily if you're relaxed. Baby will be pleased!

It's absolutely necessary to get enough rest if you're taking care of a little baby. Milk production goes better when you're rested. Even if you're bottle-feeding, your baby doesn't need an exhausted mother. *Take care of yourself.*

Breastfeeding for a Little While

You may choose to breastfeed a few days because you know how good colostrum is for your baby. If you then decide to switch to formula, both you and baby will adapt better if you don't suddenly go from full-time breastfeeding to full-time bottles.

I stopped slowly. I'd breastfeed her when she woke up at 5 a.m. because that was more convenient.

*I didn't have to get up and make a bottle. At first, I'd
give her a bottle at school, then breastfeed her at
home. Then I had less milk, and it all worked out.*

Adriana, 18 - Rachel, 3 months

Adriana was wise to stop breastfeeding gradually.
Deciding to switch baby from breast to bottle suddenly is
hard on baby and hard on mom. If you simply quit
breastfeeding one day, your body will continue producing
milk for a while. Your breasts will hurt and you might
develop a breast infection.

It's far better to give her a bottle for one of her feedings
each day for a few days, then cut out another breastfeeding,
then another, until you're feeding her from the bottle all the
time. You will both adjust to the change much better than if
you switch suddenly.

You May Prefer Bottle-Feeding

*Bottle-feeding just seemed normal to me. I was
smoking a lot, and they told me I shouldn't breastfeed
because I'd give Mona the nicotine.*

Ellie, 17 - Mona, 11 months

If you decide to bottle-feed, you can choose from ready-
to-use, concentrated, or powdered formula. The ready-to-
use formula is the most expensive and the easiest to use.
Whichever formula you choose, follow mixing instructions
carefully. Be sure bottles and nipples are absolutely clean.
Boil the water and let it cool before you mix it with either
the concentrated or powdered formula. Or you can use
bottled water. *Be sure you use the right proportion of
formula to water.*

Always check the temperature of the formula before
giving it to baby. Baby probably prefers lukewarm
formula.

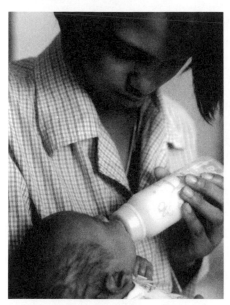

Always hold baby while you feed her,
whether by breast or bottle.

Check the size of the nipple holes occasionally. They should be just big enough so the formula drips slowly from the bottle when you hold it upside down. If the formula comes out too fast, the holes are too big. He won't get enough sucking as he drinks. The only solution is to buy new nipples.

Some babies are allergic to cow's milk. Ask your health-care provider if your baby seems to have problems. She will probably prescribe a formula made of soybean powder.

Heating baby's bottle in the microwave oven is a dangerous practice. While the bottle may feel cool, the formula inside could be hot enough to burn your baby.

Baby Needs Burping

> *Usually I feed him six ounces, and I burp him every two ounces. I place the burp rag over my left shoulder. I pat his back and rub him in a forward stroke. If he gets to where he's real colicky and cranky, I put him on his stomach and burp him that way.*
>
> Chelsea, 19 - Clancy, 2 months

Some babies need burping several times during a feeding while others don't want or need their meal interrupted. You'll be sensitive to *your* baby's needs. Several burping positions work:

• Hold her upright against your shoulder.

• Support her in a sitting position on your lap.

• Lay her on her stomach across your knees.

Whichever position you choose, rub or pat her back gently until she burps. For many babies, this happens fairly quickly, while others need several minutes of help with the important job of burping:

> *Keonia often has too much gas in her stomach.*
> *When that happens, I spend ten to twenty minutes*
> *burping her. If I don't, she'll spit up again.*
>   Lei, 16 - Keonia, 4 months

If you bottle-feed, your doctor will tell you about how much formula your baby needs. At times, baby won't finish her bottle. You don't need to worry. She probably wasn't as hungry as usual.

Her appetite will vary from feeding to feeding. "Enough" at one meal may not be enough next time. You will find she eats about the same *total* amount of formula each day.

If he has a fever or diarrhea, he needs extra water. If he has the hiccups, offer him a sip of water from a teaspoon.

Whether you breast- or bottle-feed, hold your baby close while you feed her. This is a wonderful getting-acquainted time for both of you. As you talk and smile with her, you'll feel even closer to each other.

No Propped Bottles — Ever

Whenever you give your baby a bottle, *always* be sure you hold him. Don't ever lay him down and prop his bottle in his mouth, then leave him to drink alone.

First of all, he needs the love and emotional support he'll feel from being in your arms. He also needs eye contact with you while he's eating. These happenings are all extremely important to baby.

*I blew it with my mother-in-law yesterday. She's
been wanting to keep little Eric for a few hours, and I
finally took him over there. I thought he'd be all right
while I did some shopping. I came back about two
hours later, and I couldn't believe my eyes.*

*My mother-in-law was working in the kitchen, and
there Eric was on the couch — with a bottle propped
in his mouth!*

*You should have seen him. His little hands were all
clenched, and his whole body looked tense and up-
tight. Usually when he's eating, he waves his arms
and has such a good time.*

*I was furious. I took a deep breath and said, "If
you don't have time to hold him while he eats, I do." I
picked him up and went home!*

*Babies need to be held while they're eating. They
need that love and attention. Besides, bottle-propping
is dangerous — he could choke, and it could cause an
ear infection. If she ever keeps him again, she'd better
not prop his bottle!*

Jeanne

As Jeanne said, in addition to the loving he gets from
being held while he eats, he's also less likely to have an ear
infection if you don't ever prop his bottle. Many ear infec-
tions are caused by baby drinking from a propped bottle.
The passageway from the ear to the throat doesn't drain
well in infancy. Formula, if not "served" properly, can go
back to his ears and cause an infection.

If you need another reason for holding baby while you
feed him, remember that a baby with a propped bottle can
spit up and choke on the milk curd. He's unable to spit it
out if a bottle is propped in his mouth.

He May Need a Pacifier

Babies need a lot of sucking. Breastfed babies can usually suck more while eating than bottle-fed babies. If the formula in the bottle is gone, it's gone, while the breast keeps producing a dribble of milk. A baby who needs lots of sucking can get it there.

Lots of babies, however, whether breastfed or bottle-fed, need still more sucking. Your baby may find her fist soon after birth. (Many babies suck their thumbs while still in mother's womb.) If she seems to want more sucking, offer her a pacifier.

If you're breastfeeding, as mentioned earlier, wait until she's a month old. Offer the pacifier only after she's finished nursing. *Never* let a pacifier come between baby and his meal.

Even if the neighbors frown, giving your baby a pacifier is fine. Throw it away as soon as she doesn't seem to need the extra sucking, probably before the end of the first year.

Just don't substitute the pacifier for the attention, food, or diaper change she wants and needs when she's crying.

Vitamin/Mineral Supplements

If you're breastfeeding your baby, continue taking your prenatal vitamins for two or three months after delivery. If you do, your baby won't need an extra vitamin supplement. She gets her vitamins through your milk, and an extra dose wouldn't be good for her.

Vitamins. Commercially prepared formula contains enough vitamin D for baby.

Fluoride. Whether you're breastfeeding or bottle-feeding, your baby needs fluoride. In some areas this is in the water supply. Getting enough fluoride helps prevent cavities in our teeth while too much fluoride can be a problem. It can lead to discolored teeth.

Since the amount of fluoride in your water supply may be high or low, it's important that you ask your healthcare provider how much, if any, fluoride supplement your baby needs. Give exactly as prescribed. Don't overdose!

Iron. If you're eating enough nutritious, iron-rich foods, your breast milk will provide enough iron for your baby for about four months. At that time, your healthcare provider may suggest an iron supplement. Or she may tell you it's all right to start feeding baby an iron-fortified cereal.

Most commercial formulas contain iron. Your doctor will help you decide which one is best for your baby.

Call WIC for Food Expense Help

If it's hard for you to get enough of the right foods for yourself while you're breastfeeding, call your public health department for information about WIC (Special Supplemental Feeding Program for Women, Infants, and Children). WIC also provides help in buying nutritious foods for pregnant women and for baby's formula. In some communities, WIC eligibility depends on income. Very young mothers may qualify based on age.

The food stamp program helps extend food dollars for eligible families. Ask your social worker for information.

Whether you breastfeed or feed your baby with a bottle, eating time can be a period of special closeness for the two of you. Talk to her as she eats. Tell her how much you love her. Let her know how much you like this part of your day, and she will respond more and more as the days go by.

A baby being held and fed by a loving, unhurried parent is learning that most important lesson — to trust her world and you. *Cherish the time you have together.*

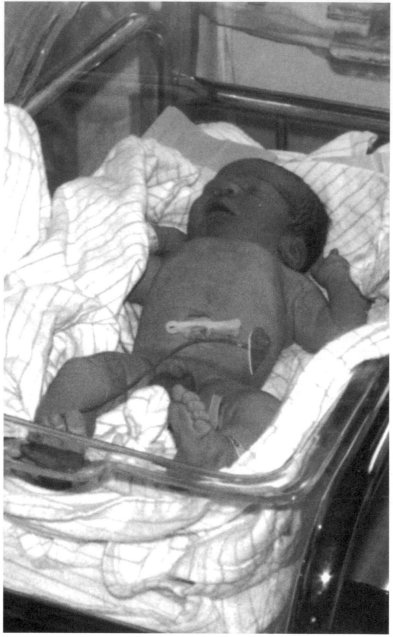

Your newborn is an extraordinary little person.

3

Observing Your Wonderful Newborn

- **Your Newborn's Appearance**

- **Taking Care of Baby's Belly Button**

- **Characteristics of Your Newborn**

- **Watching Her Develop**

- **Vision — A Bit Hazy**

- **Reflex Actions Prevail**

- **Learning from Baby**

The first time I saw Jazlyn I was so happy. I couldn't believe she was here already, that I had her in me and that she was finally out. She was so little, and she was so pretty. As soon as I saw her, I loved her already.

Tristyn, 16 - Jazlyn, 2 months

At first she was all purple and she had little pink lips like she had lipstick on. By the second day her little nose looked like it was growing, like it pushed out. When she came home I thought she looked like her dad. She has changed so much. She has big brown eyes, and is very alert.

Mia, 18 - Isabel, 6 weeks

Your Newborn's Appearance

The work of labor is not easy for either you or your baby. Your just-born baby may not look at all like the dreamy little person in the diaper commercials. She may seem stressed and look all worn out.

However, like nearly every mother, father, and grandparent, you will probably find it's love at first sight.

As soon as she came out, a weird feeling came over me, an adrenalin rush. It was neat finally to see her, having her open up her eyes and look at me.
                                    Philip, 17 - Julia, 2 months

You may notice that your baby looks pretty messy after delivery until the nurse cleans her up. The baby's head may become molded during labor and delivery, looking longer than you think it should. There may be bumps and lumps there as well.

As your baby traveled through the birth canal, her head changed slightly to make the trip a little easier. At this point, the bones in baby's head are soft enough to let this happen. Soon her head will become round. If you were in labor for a long time, your baby's head was more likely to undergo molding.

Most babies are fairly red when they're born, sometimes even purplish looking. This is true regardless of their ethnic origin. By the time you take baby home from the hospital, his skin will look better. His skin may be red and blotchy when he cries, but this is normal.

African American babies' skin is often lighter at birth than it will be later. The skin at the tip of the ear is a good indication of the baby's permanent color.

When Latrelle was born, he was real white and he had big pink lips. He had a head full of hair, and he

*still does — but his lips aren't pink and now he's
darker.*

LaTanya, 18 - Latrelle, 4 weeks

Have you heard of baby's *fontanel?* This is a "soft spot"
(actually, more than one) on the top of her head. Some
people worry that baby might be injured if the soft spot is
touched. However, a tough membrane covers the fontanel.
This gives her head plenty of protection. It takes about 18
months for the skull to close over the soft spot.

You'd be wise to check baby's soft spot. It should be
soft and flat. If it bulges or is sunken, baby may be sick or
dehydrated.

Be sure you wash baby's head thoroughly. Otherwise,
cradle cap might develop. This is scaliness similar to heavy
dandruff. When you give your baby a shampoo, just mas-
sage her head with your fingertips as you would your own.
Touching the soft spot is not going to hurt it.

Should cradle cap develop, the best way to treat it is to
wash baby's head with a low-allergy soap or clean her head
with a soft brush. You can also use baby oil. Apply it with
cotton or a soft brush. Then wash it off in a few minutes.

Taking Care of Baby's Belly Button

Parents are sometimes nervous about touching their
newborn baby's umbilical cord. It might bleed a little if
moved. If that happens, just clean it gently with alcohol on
a piece of cotton. The good news is that the cord drops off
in a week or so. Most doctors recommend that baby not be
put in water until his cord drops off.

When baby's belly button (navel) sticks out, some
parents feel that something should be done about it. How-
ever, putting binders or other objects (penny, etc.) on it can
cause the belly button to become infected. If your baby's

belly button sticks out, that's okay. As baby's tummy
muscles get stronger, her belly button will probably go in.

If your baby's belly button sticks out a lot, however, ask
your doctor to check for umbilical hernia. See page 67.

Umbilical hernia: A bulge near the belly button
where the abdominal muscles come together.

Characteristics of Your Newborn

*I wasn't used to waking up every two or three hours
to feed her, and it was hard. Sometimes when I'd feed
her, she would keep crying. The first couple of nights
were real hard, but I got used to it.*

*Now she sleeps good, although right now she wants
to be awake more. She wants people to be talking to
her. Of course I talk to her whenever she's awake.*

Tristyn, 16 - Jazlyn, 2 months

A newborn baby depends completely on her parents or
other caregivers to meet all of her needs. During the first
days of life in the world, she will probably be sleepy except
about three minutes or so per hour — this in addition to the
time she spends crying because she is hungry, wet, gener-
ally uncomfortable, or lonely, or while she's eating. During
those few minutes of "alert" time, she will be getting to
know you and the world you share.

During the first two or three days after birth, all babies
lose a few ounces. They gain this weight back within
a few days.

Newborns' first bowel movements (BMs) are called
meconium, a greenish-black sticky substance. This fills
baby's intestines while she is still in your uterus. The
meconium usually comes out during the first day or two
after birth. After that, new babies have greenish BMs that

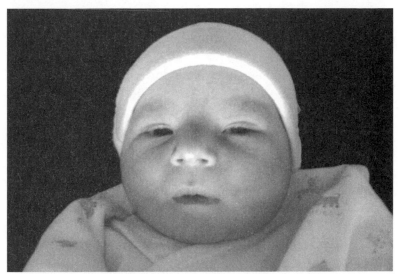

Baby loves to have you talk to her.

are soft. If that is how they look (soft and green), it doesn't matter how many they have. Breastfed babies have yellowish stools after each feeding. The quickly digested breast milk results in this event, and it's good for baby.

It is quite normal for some babies, both boys and girls, to have swollen breasts for a few days after delivery. Caused by the hormones from the mother's body, this will go away within a few days. Occasionally baby's breast will contain a little milk. Do not try to squeeze it out.

Mother's hormones may also cause girl babies to have a slight amount of bleeding from the vagina for two or three days after delivery. Both boy and girl babies have oversized genitals which appear red at birth. They will gradually become smaller in the first week or two. It is also normal and nothing to worry about if a boy baby gets an erect penis when you change his diaper. This often occurs throughout early childhood.

Some babies have birthmarks. Many will disappear in time. These marks tend to run in families, and you can do

nothing to make them go away. If you are concerned, ask
your health care provider about it during a well baby
checkup.

Dark-skinned babies may have dark-colored marks,
often on or above the buttocks. These fade by about the
child's second birthday.

Milia or baby acne develops in some newborns. This,
too, is due to a hormonal imbalance. These little
whiteheads disappear in a couple of weeks. No treatment is
needed. Be sure not to use adult acne medicines on baby.

Watching Her Develop

> *When I first saw him, I cried. It was something that*
> *nobody could take away from me. He was really pink,*
> *and he had blond hair. He was wide-eyed already.*
> *They usually say the baby comes out groggy after the*
> *epidural, but he was trying to look everywhere.*
>
> Zaria, 16 - Devyn, 3 months

When you pay more attention to baby, she will pay more
attention to you. Knowing more about the wonderful
process of how a baby develops will make it more special
when the two of you spend that "alert" time together, and
she begins to respond.

From the very first sight you have of your baby, his look
and behavior will be unlike any of the other babies in the
nursery. Your baby may be awake and alert more than
others, or he may sleep "all the time." Fall in love with
your baby just as he is.

Babies usually respond to sounds at birth. (Most babies
born in the United States will have a hearing test before
they leave the hospital.) Startling at loud noises is quite
normal, and baby may even cry.

While she doesn't understand the meaning of all your
words, she *loves* to hear your voice. It sounds and feels

Most newborns sleep a lot those first few days —
and Mom needs to sleep, too!

familiar like the time she spent in your uterus. Singing and
talking to babywill make her pay close attention you. How-
ever, loud, sharp noises and angry voices will upset her.

Vision — A Bit Hazy

Seeing well is not something that the baby has devel-
oped at birth. You probably look hazy to him when you're
more than nine inches away. This is about the distance the
baby's eyes are from yours while breastfeeding.

Since baby's eye muscles are not fully developed at
birth, her eyes may sometimes even seem "crossed." Within
a few weeks, muscle development will improve and this
will go away.

Eye color generally is not the same after a few months as
it was at birth. Many babies have blue or gray eyes when
they're born, and later develop darker or lighter eyes. Some
babies are born with dark eyes, but even the shade or
darkness may change over time.

You are your baby's favorite object of attention. She will follow your movements for a short distance soon after birth. Sometime before she's two months old, she will smile at you — and you will never forget it. Earlier, she will smile, but some people say this is only a reflex. That smile occurs when baby is content. Often she is awake when it happens.

Suggestions

• Some infant toys have unbreakable mirrors as part of them. Place the toy in a position where baby sees herself. Since she prefers faces, this will interest her longer than another toy.

• Draw a face on a paper plate using dark markers or crayons. Attach the plate to the crib about ten inches from baby's face. Put it on the side of the crib where she most likes to look.

Reflex Actions Prevail

Reflexes already developed at birth cause many of a newborn baby's actions:

Reflex action: Responding to something without having to learn to do so.

You will notice your hungry baby turning her head and "looking" for the breast. That reflex is called rooting. Once she has found the breast (or bottle), she will know how to suck, which is another reflex.

When your baby is awake, he won't always be quiet. He will be experiencing a variety of things that are a part of his immature nervous system. Examples are the hiccup, startling, and shaking. Young mothers are often concerned by these behaviors, but this is quite okay.

During the first week or so, your baby will take "steps" when you hold her in a standing position. This is another reflex, and it lasts only briefly. Later, when you try the same thing, baby will sag down rather than take "steps." All of this is normal.

Another surprising thing parents notice is the strength of baby's grip. During the first month or so the baby's hands are in a fist as a reflex position. Later baby's hands relax, and he will start to explore them.

Pictures of newborn babies almost always show them bundled up in blankets. During the first few hours after birth, babies are warmed up to help them adjust to the temperature of the world outside their mother. But after the first day or so, a baby needs the same amount of clothing layers that you do, which will vary from indoors to out-doors. When you need a coat or sweater, dress baby accordingly. If your baby develops a prickly heat rash, she is too warm.

Learning from Baby

As you are around other babies, you begin to see how different each baby is from the others. Some pass mile-stones of development before others. Personality traits such as being very quiet or very active begin to show up. As you notice these things, share your observations with others who love your baby. You may even want to start a baby book by writing down things you notice. It will be fun for him to hear about his early milestones and read your first notes about him.

Most of all, enjoy this wonderful time. You are the most important person in your baby's life — and he in yours.

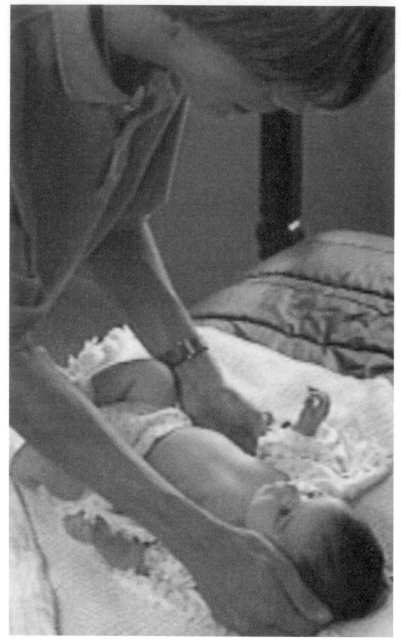

Your baby depends on you to keep him as comfortable as possible.

4

Baby's Goal — To Be Comfortable

How do I comfort Cassidy? I pick him up and I talk to him, and he settles down.

Sumaire, 17 - Cassidy, 6 weeks

If she's upset, it could be because she has a dirty diaper or she's hungry or tired. When she's tired, I start patting her back, and it relaxes her and she falls asleep.

She likes to be warm, and we make sure she's warm. When we feed her, we put a blanket around her and hold her tight.

When we first pick her up and she's all fussy, we hold her real close to us. Then she starts to realize, "Okay, I'm comfortable."

Mike, 18 - Isabel, 6 weeks

Meeting Baby's Needs

Comfort is the most important thing to a newborn. Comfort first of all means having her needs met. Letting her "cry it out" makes sense only when you can't do anything to help her feel better. Even then, most babies prefer to be held in their misery. Wouldn't you?

Nearly every baby loves to be touched, held, and cuddled. They have a way of snuggling into your arms that makes both you and baby feel good. When baby is fussy, holding her upright with her head near your shoulder may quiet her.

Your new baby is extremely sensitive. A loud noise or somebody jolting her bassinet may make her cry. She may even cry if you lift her suddenly from her bed. In fact, she may startle and cry at any sudden change.

Put your hands carefully under her, then wait a second or two before you pick her up. This way, she'll feel more secure. It gives her time to adjust to being moved. Naturally you always provide head support for a young baby whenever you lift her or hold her.

You Can't "Spoil" Your Infant

When she cries, I pick her up. My mom says, "If you don't lay her down when she sleeps, she'll be used to you holding her." When she's older, my mom says I'll have to hold her. But I don't think she'll do that.

LaTasha, 16 - Tajanell, 6 weeks

Spoiling your baby is *not* something that's going to happen these first few months. Most parents love holding their baby, so touch her and love her. This gives her a secure feeling about her life.

Your baby, like all babies, was born with 100 billion brain cells just waiting to develop. His brain cells will develop though stimulation, like lights and sound (especially the sound of his parents' voices). Touch is so important that babies who are rarely touched or played with have smaller brains! Your baby's brain will develop the most during his first three years after birth.

Sometimes grandparents — or other people around the baby — think picking him up will spoil him. Perhaps someone has said to you, "If you pick him up every time he cries, he'll think he can get whatever he wants by crying." True, he'll cry when he needs something, whether you pick him up or not. And he *needs* to be picked up and have his needs met as much as possible.

The parent who answers his cries is helping him develop that all-important trust in his world. In fact, that sense of trust is the most important thing he can learn during his first months.

Did you know that research actually shows that babies who are often picked up and held during their first months cry *less* when they are a year old? Yes, infants who are more often left alone as they cry will cry *more* when they're older.

So follow your heart. Pick up your baby, talk to her, sing to her, cuddle her. Feed her when she's hungry. Keep her clean, warm (but not *too* warm) and dry. You'll both be ahead if baby gets the attention she needs.

I usually hold her, rub her face, play with her feet. She'll just look up at me. Now she smiles. Just talking about her makes me miss her.

Philip, 17 - Julia, 2 months

Talk with him *a lot.* He will learn more easily later than will the child who spends these early months lying in a crib or sitting in an infant seat not doing much of anything. So *keep talking!*

Enjoying Your Baby

When Jenilee cries I pick her up and hold her
against my chest with her face where she can hear my
heart beat. She likes me to walk around with her. Or I
start talking with her. She likes to listen to my voice.

Lacey, 16 - Jenilee, 1 month

The most important part of caring for your baby is
getting to know her — bonding together as closely as
possible. If you interact a lot with baby, hold her, talk to
her, carry on conversations whenever she's awake, you'll
find the bonding happens just the way it should.

Focus on your newborn's comfort. When he's hungry,
he wants and needs to be fed *now*. He may hate wet or
messy diapers, or he may not seem to notice. If he doesn't
like them, he lets you know by crying. Even if you've fed
and changed him, and you know he's neither too warm nor
too cold, he may still cry. He may be a colicky baby who
just cries more than some babies do. (See page 61.)

If she cries after being fed, is it possible she still needs
burping? Most babies can burp when you rub or pat their
backs gently for a minute or two. Others need to have their
backs patted or rubbed for a longer time. (See pages 31-32.)

Don't worry about spoiling him. Being there when he
needs you helps him learn to trust his world. If he trusts his
needs will be met, he's likely to cry less in the future.

Important Note

Sometimes you'll do everything you can to help your
baby be comfortable, and she'll still cry. Always remember
she is not crying to upset you. She isn't crying because
you've spoiled her. She's crying because it's the only way
she can tell you that she needs you.

Sometimes taking her outside will help. She may stop

crying if she has something new and different to watch. A ride in the car (safely secured in her car seat) may calm her. Some mothers report their babies fall asleep almost the instant the car starts.

Some babies go to sleep most easily when they're in their swing. Soft music might help. A little music box beside their bed soothes some babies.

Does He Cry Because He's Lonely?

The first two weeks are the hardest. He woke up every hour, and it was very frustrating for me. After about two weeks he started waiting two hours before he'd wake up, but he still doesn't fall asleep until 2 a.m. I'm still very tired.

Tiana, 15 - Francisco, 3 months

Does your baby sometimes cry when "there's nothing wrong with him"? You've fed him, you've changed his diaper, and you know he's not too hot or too cold. Still he cries.

He may simply be lonely. What do you suppose it feels like to move from the warm comfort of his mother's uterus to the outside world? Do you think you'd suddenly want to sleep by yourself with no human touch? That's quite a change for baby.

Be patient with your baby. There are times when they cry, and you think they're hungry and they don't want the bottle. Something else is bothering her. Like Jazlyn, she doesn't like to have a wet or dirty diaper. And sometimes she's lonely.

Tristyn, 16 - Jazlyn, 2 months

Don't be afraid to hold her even if you know she's not hungry, wet or cold. Hopefully, you have a rocking chair. Use it! Most babies also like a rocking cradle. Sing or croon to her as you rock her.

Perhaps you can't afford both an expensive crib and a rocking chair. Your baby would undoubtedly vote for a cheap unpainted or used crib so you could also buy the rocking chair.

Bathing Your Newborn

Until your baby's umbilical cord drops off, she shouldn't be put in water. Just give her a "sponge" bath. Lay her on a towel in a warm room and wash her with a soapy washcloth. Then rinse her off thoroughly and dry her.

After the cord drops off, you can give baby a real bath. Wash his head and face first. Don't use soap on his face, but wash his hair with plain soap or baby shampoo at least once a week. After you've washed and dried his face, use your hand to lather the rest of his body with plain soap. Wash the baby's genitals just as you do the rest of his body. Rinse him thoroughly, wrap him in a towel, and pat him dry. Be sure you talk to him the entire time.

> *When I gave her her first bath I was scared. I*
> *bathed her in a little tub thing in the sink. She didn't*
> *cry the first time, perhaps because she was used to*
> *being inside the womb. When I finished I wrapped her*
> *in a whole bunch of towels. She was still slippery.*
>
> LaTasha, 16 - Tajanell, 6 weeks

If your kitchen sink is big enough, you might prefer to bathe your baby there. It's a comfortable height, and you don't have to lift the tub to empty the water. You have to be extra careful not to let baby slip and get hurt on the faucets.

If you live in a family home with a lot of different people, however, using the sink may interfere with their routine. If you do wash baby in the sink, clean it thoroughly before and after her bath.

Always test the water to be sure it isn't too hot. Stick your elbow in it. It's more sensitive to temperature than your hands are.

Never leave baby alone in her bath.

> *First bath? He didn't like it. He screamed and cried and it scared me. I still haven't found a good technique because he doesn't like to take baths.*
>
> *For the first month and a half I just gave him a sponge bath like I did when he was first born. He doesn't mind that. My mom and my grandmother think it's kind of silly. They thought I should just give him a bath, but I feel whatever works for me and him is the best thing so . . . the sponge bath worked well.*
>
> Brooke, 18 - Blair, 3 months

Even though some infants find bath time relaxing and soothing, a lot of tiny babies don't like their bath. Sometimes when you put her in the water, she may shiver. If she does, shorten her bath, then wrap her in a towel. And there's nothing wrong with bathing a baby by using a washcloth to wash her while she lies on the towel, as Brooke did. And babies don't *have* to have a bath every day.

Of course you'll clean her bottom thoroughly when you change her. A daily bath is a nice part of her routine — if she's okay about it. If she hates it, bathe her every other day, perhaps only a sponge bath for a little longer.

Don't try to clean any body opening (nose, ears, navel) with cotton-tipped sticks. Anything you can't clean with a corner of a washcloth doesn't need cleaning. You don't need to use cream, lotion, or powder on baby's body either. In fact, some of these products may irritate her skin. Clean babies smell good without the help of these items.

Don't worry when your baby touches his/her genitals.

S/he's curious about this part of his/her body. Touching the genitals is as normal and certainly as harmless as touching one's nose.

The Diaper Question

Disposable diapers seem to be used "by everyone." They're easy to use, and often are considered simply another necessary expense of baby care. It's still possible, however, to buy cloth diapers and wash them yourself. You'd spend less money. Cloth diapers are also kinder to our environment.

> *I use cloth diapers because of the money. Every week I had to buy a bag of diapers — nearly $100 a month! For 88 diapers it's over $20. I started using cloth when he was two or three months old.*
>
> *I think a lot of girls use the disposables because they're lazy. They think changing cloth diapers is gross. Sometimes they're afraid they'll stick the baby with the pins. I use the cloth kind with the velcro.*
>
> Delia, 15 - Kelsey, 7 months

Before you decide whether to use a diaper service, disposables, or diapers you wash yourself, figure out the comparative cost in your area.

Most of us would find several hundred extra dollars quite welcome at the end of the year. That's the difference in cost between using disposable diapers or the wash-your-own kind. If you have good laundry facilities, washing diapers isn't hard. And you can always fold them while you watch television.

> *I use cloth diapers. I don't like disposables. Robin gets rashes from paper and not from cloth diapers. If you rinse them out, they don't stink. I put them in the*

*washer before school, and put them in the dryer when
I get home. I fold them after she goes to sleep.*

Melinda, 15 - Robin, 9 months

Does She Like to Be Swaddled?

*When Jazlyn was a newborn, we put her on a blanket
and I'd wrap the blanket real tight. I'd do that when I was
feeding her or when she was sleeping.*

Now she wants to have her hands free.

Tristyn

Do you swaddle your baby? This means wrapping him
tightly in a blanket. This is common in many cultures.
Perhaps it works because baby feels more secure if he's
wrapped snugly. This may help him feel more like he felt in
your uterus. He was "wrapped" quite snugly there!

To swaddle a baby, center her on the blanket with her
head just over one edge. Pick up an upper corner of the
blanket and bring it down diagonally over her shoulder. Her
elbow will be inside, but one hand should be free. Tuck the
corner under baby's knees.

Pull up the other side of the blanket and fold it snugly
over baby. Lift her a little so you can put the edge of the
blanket under her.

You'll have a snugly wrapped baby, and you may have a
more contented baby. In fact, some infants will sleep better
if they're swaddled as they're put to bed.

Your newborn baby is already an interesting little person
who knows more than people used to believe. Already
you're a big influence on your baby's behavior. Love her,
teach her.

Above all, enjoy your time together.

---

*For more information, see **Your Baby and Child
from Birth to Age Five** by Penelope Leach (Knopf).*

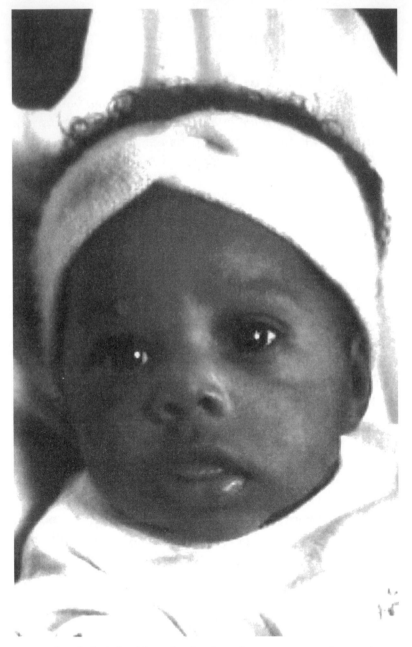

Guarding baby's health and safety is an important part of parenting.

5

Guarding Your Infant's Health and Safety

Julia has an ear infection. Normally she sleeps all the time. Once she started staying awake and she was cranky, we figured she was sick.

We took her to the doctor and he prescribed medicine for the ear infection. Now it's clearing up.

Philip, 17 - Julia, 2 months

Francisco was congested for about two weeks. He was coughing and gagging a lot, and every two minutes, I'd have to clean out his nose with a bulb syringe. I felt so sorry for him, but he's okay now.

Tiana, 15 - Francisco, 3 months

Note: If your baby was born prematurely or has other
special needs, please see chapter 9, *Your Pregnancy and
Newborn Journey,* for additional health care information.

Her First Doctor's Appointment

Health care is changing. Families may have their health
care provided by a doctor, nurse practitioner, a physician's
assistant, or other specialist. These people are sometimes
referred to as *healthcare providers.* Both "doctor" and
"healthcare provider" are used here to mean health
professional.

You probably selected your baby's doctor/medical plan
before your child was born. Healthcare providers generally
have you bring the baby in when she's about two weeks
old, sometimes much sooner. At this visit it's good to talk
about any troubles at all with feeding. If you have concerns
with the baby's navel (belly button), if you suspect hernia,
or if you have other worries, tell your healthcare provider.

It's a good idea on your first visit to the healthcare
provider to learn the names of the various people working
there. If you know the names of the receptionist and the
nurse, you can call them by name when you telephone. If
you do so, you're more likely to get a friendly response.

Above all, don't be afraid to ask questions. Write down
everything you want to discuss with your healthcare pro-
vider. Is he always in a hurry? Stop him and say, "Wait. I
have these questions, and I need your help."

If you briefly describe whatever is worrying you, he'll
take time to advise you. If he doesn't, perhaps you need to
look for another doctor who will answer your questions.

You are the case manager for your child's medical
needs. Keep all the information together in a notebook so
you can grab it when you take your baby to the doctor.

Some mothers keep this notebook in the car so they'll be sure to have it with them.

Start with recording your baby's length and weight at birth and periodically thereafter. If you know your baby's blood type, write it down. Most important is to keep a record of your child's immunizations. You'll need to have this record when he starts school.

Write down the dates of your child's illnesses and briefly describe symptoms. This will help you provide information to your healthcare provider.

Be sure to keep the notebook up to date. If you're in a managed healthcare plan, you may see a different doctor each time you go. With the notebook, you'll communicate better with the doctor. He will treat you differently because you'll be seen as a capable young parent. That's better for both you and your baby.

If Baby Has Jaundice

Mia noticed Isabel was looking kind of yellow. When we took her back for her two-day check-up, the doctor said she had jaundice. It was hard for us because this was our baby, and we didn't want anything to happen to her.

We took her down to the lab, and they took blood from her. They called later and said she was on the borderline. They said to make sure she ate and pooped, and to get her in the sun by a window for half an hour each day.

We'd undress her except for her diaper and put her in the sun for 15-30 minutes. Gradually the jaundice started to disappear. Within a week she was back to a normal skin color, and her eyes were back to normal.

Mike, 18 - Isabel, 6 weeks

Thirty to fifty percent of all full-term and eighty percent

of premature babies develop jaundice. This causes their skin or the whites of their eyes to get yellowish. There are several causes, most of which have to do with the baby's immaturity.

Should your baby look yellowish, check with the doctor. Extra blood tests will be given, and the treatment could be as simple as feeding baby more often. Occasionally, special lights may be used to get rid of the yellow skin color.

The best treatment for jaundice that first week is to breastfeed often, at least every 11/2-2 hours. Put your baby near a window to sleep during the day because daylight helps the baby get rid of jaundice. Don't put baby in direct sunlight, however. If the room is warm enough, dress baby only in a diaper so the light can get to his skin.

Thrush Can Affect Infants

The visiting nurse said, "I think she has thrush on her tongue." She told me to get to the doctor for treatment. At first I was all scared because this is the first thing she'd had.

They gave me a prescription and said to apply it on the insides of her cheeks inside her mouth. They said it was okay if she swallowed it.

A couple of days later she had a diaper rash, and they said it was connected to the thrush. They gave me the same medicine, but in an ointment. The rash cleared up right away.

LaTasha, 16 - Tajanell, 6 weeks

Thrush looks like patches of milk scum on the tongue and inside the cheeks or on the roof of the mouth. Unlike milk, it does not wipe off easily. If the patches don't wipe off, call your doctor. Treatment will be simple.

This can also cause a diaper rash. This, too, can be easily cleared up with medication.

Babies and Colic

She had colic when she was little, about two hours
at night. I figured out what made her calm. Like about
a half-hour into her crying, after carrying her around,
I would give her a bath. The water calmed her down.
You have to find what she wants, like finding an itch.

Aimee, 17 - Amelia, 10 months

Some babies cry and cry, and it seems impossible to comfort them. Such a baby may have colic. If he does, he may seem to have a stomach-ache and have attacks of crying nearly every evening. His face may suddenly become red; he'll frown, draw up his legs, and scream loudly. When you pick him up to comfort him, he keeps screaming, perhaps for 15 to 20 minutes. Just as he is about to fall asleep, he may start screaming again. He may pass gas.

When Navaeh was two weeks old, she had colic
for two days. Then she got over it. She was yelling,
and I knew something was wrong because she
rarely cries. She would kick and move around.
When I'd feed her, she'd still cry, and her stomach
was hard.

Allegra, 17 - Navaeh, 6 weeks

No one knows what causes colic. It generally comes at about the same time every day. During the rest of the day, the colicky baby will probably be happy, alert, eat well, and gain weight.

If your baby seems to have colic, check with your doctor to see if anything else is wrong. If not, make sure baby isn't hungry, wet, cold, or lonely. During an attack of colic, holding him on his stomach across your knees may comfort him. Sometimes giving him a warm bath helps. There are also some medicines that may help. Ask your doctor.

The good news about colic is that baby will grow out of

it by the time he is about three months old. In the mean-
time, he will be harder to live with because of his colic.
Comfort him as best you can, and look forward to the time
his colic ends.

Dealing with Diaper Rash

The best way to deal with diaper rash is to prevent it as
much as possible. During the first month or two, change
baby before every feeding, more often if he has a bowel
movement. Some diapers agree with certain skins better
than others, so try different brands. (Start with the cheaper
ones.) Or use cloth diapers.

Change your baby often. Wash her with clean warm
water or wipes when you change her. Pat her dry, espe-
cially in the skin creases. The main cause of diaper rash is
the ammonia in the urine coming in contact with air. If she
gets a rash, it's even more important to wash her
thoroughly each time you change her.

If you have a baby girl, always wipe from front to back
to keep germs from getting into her vagina. If you have a
boy, clean around his penis and his genitals. If he's not
circumcised, don't try to pull the foreskin of his penis back
to clean him. It will be several years before the foreskin is
loose enough to pull back for cleaning underneath. Just
clean the exposed areas.

If he was circumcised, follow your doctor's advice on
caring for the circumcised area. It should heal in a week.

*The first week I used baby wipes, and he looked
like he was getting a diaper rash. I started cleaning
him with a washcloth, and the redness went away.*
                                        LaTanya, 18 - Latrelle, 4 weeks

It isn't necessary to use baby powder. If you do, it may
cake in skin creases and cause soreness. Even more

important, don't shake it directly on baby. Instead, if you must use it, put a little in your hand first, then pat it on the baby. Baby powder shaken in the air can hurt baby's lungs.

There are both prescription and non-prescription remedies for diaper rash. You can get these either as powder or ointment. The ointment gives longer protection.

If baby has a bad diaper rash, let her go without a diaper as much as possible. If she's warm enough, let her nap without a diaper. The air on the rash will help clear it up. You can protect her bed with waterproof sheeting.

To repeat, it's easier to prevent diaper rash than it is to get rid of it. For your baby's comfort — and your peace of mind — change her often. And clean her thoroughly each time you change her.

Some diaper rashes occur when a baby is taking an antibiotic. Tell your healthcare provider. She may recommend a special cream to use each time you change her.

Importance of Immunizations

Sometimes babies are sick. They have colds, fevers, and other illnesses. Later in this chapter, you will find suggestions for dealing with these usually minor illnesses.

There are other serious childhood diseases, diseases that your child need never have. It's up to you because your healthcare provider can immunize him against such diseases.

During the first eighteen months it is important to be sure your baby's immunization schedule is followed. In the past many babies died in the first year or two of life from serious illnesses that now can be prevented by these immunizations.

Now, during baby's first month, make an appointment for his first series. Here's what your child will need:

• **Hepatitis B** is given in a series of three injections.

Usually the first is given on baby's first day after birth, the second at one to two months, and the last one at six months. Baby must have all three.

• **Diphtheria, Tetanus, Pertussis (DTaP)** is also given in a series of three at two, four, and six months with a booster (Td) between 15 and 18 months.

• **H. influenzae, type b (Hib)** is another series of three. This is often given in the same injection as the DTaP and is then called HDTaP.

• **Pneumococcal** prevents a type of pneumonia common with young infants. It is given at 2, 4, and 6 months.

• **Polio (IPV)** is a red liquid given by mouth or injection at two and four months. A third dose is given between six and 18 months.

While this may seem like a lot for baby, it is important to remember that all of these diseases can cause death or very serious illness in children. When I (Jean B.) was a young nurse, I remember having a baby cough himself to death in my arms from pertussis. I felt especially sad because even then his death could have been prevented if he had been immunized. *Don't take a chance with your baby!*

As mentioned, it is also *very important* to keep the records of your child's immunizations. If you lose your record, get another one right away. When your child starts school, the school will insist on having this information. It may be hard to get it several years later.

Immunizations are free at the health department. They may be given by the health department at local parks. If you don't know where to take your baby for his shots, ask your school nurse for a recommendation.

For more detailed information about your baby's immunizations, see *Your Baby's First Year* by Lindsay.

Calling Baby's Doctor

*You call the doctor when you don't know what to
do because there's something wrong with the baby.
He might get upset if you overdo it — mine did once,
but better safe than sorry.*

*Sometimes, if I'm worried but don't think there's
much wrong, I go to another mother before I call the
doctor. If Robin has a fever or seems sick, I call.*

Melinda, 15 - Robin, 9 months

When should you call your baby's healthcare provider?
If you take baby's temperature under his arm (safer and less
disturbing to the baby than sticking a thermometer into his
rectum), and it reads more than 101 degrees, call.

The best way to take underarm (called axillary) tempera-
ture is with a disposable or digital thermometer. These are
available in drugstores. If possible, use them to take baby's
temperature. Otherwise, use a glass thermometer.

If your baby gets a sudden unexplained rash, call your
healthcare provider.

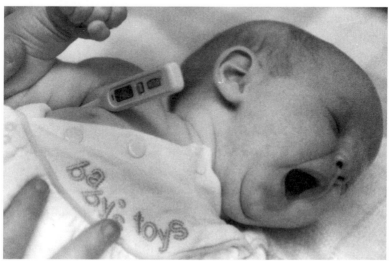

Taking underarm temperature with a digital thermometer works well.

Many babies spit up occasionally during the first two months. This is generally a combination of lumps of partially digested milk combined with watery-looking fluid. They do this because their digestive tract is not completely mature. This happens more often with premature babies. He will spit up less if you give him frequent small feedings and handle him extra gently after feeding.

Generally, this occasional spitting up is nothing to worry about. But if baby, after every feeding, suddenly vomits most of his meal, call his healthcare provider immediately.

Before you call your doctor, make some notes about your baby's condition. Then you'll be able to describe his symptoms more accurately:

- Is he coughing? For how long?
- Has he lost his appetite?
- Does he have diarrhea?
- What is his temperature?
- Has he been exposed to any diseases? Has he received the immunizations he should have had by this time?

If your healthcare provider prescribes medication for your baby, be sure to ask if you should give baby all the medicine that's in the bottle, or if you give it only for a certain number of days.

Diarrhea Can Be Serious

Diarrhea can be a serious problem for a baby. It is not diagnosed by the number of bowel movements the baby has each day. More important is the consistency of the BM.

Diarrhea: a thin, watery, foul-smelling discharge

If baby has this condition for as long as twelve hours, call the healthcare provider. A baby with diarrhea can quickly lose a dangerous amount of fluid. Check his fontanelle (soft spot). A sunken fontanelle may indicate a serious problem.

Diarrhea is best treated by giving the baby clear liquids and nothing else for 24 hours. Liquids you should give him include Pedialyte (non-prescription liquid you buy in the drugstore or grocery store), clear water, or water mixed with apple juice (one tablespoon apple juice to 8 ounces of water). Feed him liquids as often as he'll take them. If you're breastfeeding, continue to do so.

Hernia? Check with Doctor

If you think your baby might have a hernia, check with your healthcare provider.

Hernia: a bulge around the navel or the seamline between the leg and the tummy

---

You're most likely to notice it after baby has cried a lot or strained to have a bowel movement. Sometimes it will go away by itself, but occasionally it requires simple surgery. If your doctor recommends surgery, it's usually done during the second year of baby's life.

Dealing with Fever

Fever is one of the early signs of illness in a baby, and you shouldn't ignore it. What can you do about fever at home? Give the baby Tylenol or other non-aspirin pain reliever as recommended by your doctor.

Cooling baths are another way to bring fever down. If baby shivers while you're bathing him, it's too cold. A good way to do this is to put a towel in lukewarm water. Then wrap the baby in the wet towel. It helps bring his temperature down, and he's less likely to shiver.

Lukewarm water is the best thing to use. Don't use alcohol. The fumes can be dangerous for baby to breathe.

It's also important to give your child liquids when he has a fever. If it's a sore throat that's causing his fever, your baby may not want to do a lot of sucking.

That one throat infection Lynn had was terrible. I took her to the doctor, and they gave me Penicillin to give her.

She was really sick — she couldn't keep anything down. She couldn't suck the bottle because her throat was so sore. She cried a lot. We'd go to sleep, and she'd wake up 15 minutes later. Her crying got on my nerves, but when I picked her up, she'd quit crying.
                                        Sheryl Ann, 17 - Lynn, 7 months

When your baby has an ear infection, call your healthcare provider. While a non-aspirin pain reliever can take away some of the pain and the fever, it doesn't kill the germs causing the infection in the ear.

On one of your first visits, ask the doctor what to do if your baby gets an ear infection. Some healthcare providers want to see the baby right away. Others may recommend some things you can try first such as a decongestant. Do whatever is recommended, but don't ignore this illness.

As discussed in chapter 2, many infants' ear infections are caused by propped bottles.

Colds Are Common

Most children catch a few colds during their first two years. Colds are most contagious the first couple of days, sometimes before the carrier knows he's sick, so it's impossible to protect your child completely from getting colds.

When Evan was three weeks old, he caught his first cold. Marlene kept a record of those days:

9/4: Today Evan has a slight cough. I hope it doesn't get worse.

9/5: Evan got the sniffles and his cough is worse. When I feed him, he'll cough, and it seems like he's choking. It scares me.

9/6: Evan's cold is getting worse. His nose is plugged. I called the doctor, and she told me to use normal saline and put it in his nose because he has a hard time breathing. I'm gonna take him to the doctor tomorrow because I want to make sure. My mom is helping me out.

9/8: Today Evan woke up around 9:00 and slept through most of the day. He's still coughing. His sniffles are getting a little better but he still gets plugged up from time to time. During the night, as usual, he's a grouch, but I finally got him to sleep by holding him in my arms and singing to him like I usually do.

9/9: Evan is a month old. He stays awake a lot. I don't mind that. It's the crying I could live without.

9/10: I wish his cold would go away. The doctor said we can't give him any medication because he's too young. I feel so sorry for him because it seems like he's having such a hard time.

9/12: He's still sick. He stays up so much, and he's always crying. I hate his cold. I don't have time these past few days to do anything because he's always awake and crying because he doesn't feel good.

9/14: Finally he's feeling better.

Neither you nor your healthcare provider can "cure" your child's cold — there is no known cure. You can help him be more comfortable. If he has a fever or headache, Tylenol may help.

If he has a runny or stuffy nose, use normal saline and a

bulb syringe to clean the discharge from baby's nose.
Normal saline is available from the drugstore without a
prescription. The hospital probably gave you a bulb syringe
for this purpose for baby.

Decongestant medicine may also make him feel better. If
his nose is sore, cream or ointment on the area is soothing.

If he's coughing, your doctor may recommend cough
medicine. If he has a stuffy nose, a cold-mist humidifier
will help him breathe more easily. The old-fashioned steam
vaporizers are dangerous, and they don't work as well.

If he doesn't want to eat, don't worry. When he's feeling
better, he'll be hungry again. Encourage him to drink water.

How often your child has a cold depends on two things:
the number of people with colds to whom he is exposed,
and his own resistance.

Stuffy noses can be due to allergies. If a mother smokes
during pregnancy, her baby is at greater risk for developing
asthma and other allergies. When an infant or child
breathes second-hand smoke, it can have the same effect. A
smoke-free home is a wonderful gift to give your child. Not
having to breathe smoke means he's less likely to get sick
with a respiratory problem.

A lot of allergies disappear in time as baby becomes
more adjusted to life on the outside. Therefore, most doc-
tors don't start serious allergy testing until a child is much
older, usually school age.

Keeping your baby as healthy as possible is one of the
challenges of parenthood. First, do all you can to ensure
she has a good diet, gets plenty of sleep, and receives other
good physical care in addition to an unending supply
of love.

When she doesn't feel well, call your healthcare
provider. Help her be as comfortable as possible. Hope-
fully, she will soon be her happy, active self again.

Keeping Baby Safe

Accident-proofing your home is *absolutely* essential if you have a baby, toddler, or preschooler living there. Accidents injure and kill many young children every year. Keeping your child safe is one of your biggest challenges.

Never leave baby alone on a changing table, bed, or other off-the-floor surface for a second. The baby who couldn't turn over yesterday may do so today.

When you visit friends, put your tiny baby's blanket on the floor. She can nap there as well as she could on the bed, and she'll be much safer. She can't fall off the floor. Be sure she's protected from house pets and small children.

Your baby should not have a pillow in her bed. A pillow could cause a breathing problem if she got her face buried in it. If grandma made a beautifully embroidered pillow for her, appreciate it, but keep it out of her crib.

Until she can turn over by herself, always lay baby on her back to sleep. This lessens the danger of SIDS (Sudden Infant Death Syndrome).

A propped bottle is dangerous for infants. Baby could choke from her formula coming too fast from that propped bottle. She could also choke on milk curds if she should spit up. She might be unable to clear her throat.

Never leave your baby alone in the house, even if you're sure she's sound asleep. And *never* leave him alone in the car!

Making sure your infant is safe in your home, in your car, everywhere he goes, is a big responsibility. Know that, at this point, your baby depends on you for *everything*!

Baby and Dad are bonding together.

6

Dad's a Parent, Too

I was excited. For so long Mia and I were rubbing her stomach and talking to the baby — and then finally Isabel was born. It was a joy I'll never forget. I was there from the contractions to the time she was born, and I stayed in the hospital with her and Mia.

It was kind of rough. We weren't used to somebody waking us up in the middle of the night.

Taking her home was exciting. I stayed at Mia's house the first night. After that I'd go home about 1 a.m. I was kind of jealous because Mia got to stay 24 hours with the baby. I wanted to be there.

Mike, 18 - Isabel, 6 weeks

Everyone Wins If Dad's Involved

Many young mothers parent their child alone. This book is written for them. It is *also* written for:

- Young couples who are parenting their child together.
- Young fathers involved with their child, or would like to be, whether or not they're "with" their child's mom.
- Teen fathers who are parenting alone.

If you and your baby's mother aren't married, it's important that you establish paternity. This means that you both sign legal papers stating that you are the father of your child. If you don't, your child might not be able to claim Social Security, insurance benefits, veteran's and other types of benefits through you.

Your child needs your love and care. He also needs your financial support. Both parents are required by law to support their child.

What Are Your Rights?

What if you're the father, but your baby's mother doesn't want you to see your baby? You need to know your rights.

If you're providing some financial support — and usually even if you're not — you have a right to see your baby. Legally, you may be able to have your child with you part of the time. Parents who disagree on this matter should talk to a lawyer or legal aid group.

Have you declared paternity? To repeat, this is an important step whether or not you and the mother are together.

Fathers have a right to see their child, and sometimes they need to take the initiative. It's a good idea to keep a record of your visits with your child. Get written receipts for the money you provide for child support. This information could help if you ever need to prove in court your interest in your child.

A Father's Responsibilities

It's important that you do all you can to support your family financially. You probably need to get a job as soon as possible. Continuing your education, however, is also extremely important.

Do you have health insurance? If so, check to see if it covers your baby, too.

Sometimes fathers have jealous feelings after their baby is born. Your partner may seem totally absorbed in the baby and have no time left for you. Perhaps she seems exhausted much of the time. Your best defense is to be as involved as possible with her in caring for your child.

If she plans to breastfeed your baby, she'll need your encouragement and support. See chapter 2.

Even if you can't offer financial support now, you can be involved in the care of your child. If you're both in school, you may need to set up a schedule for child care which will allow time for each of you to do your homework.

Sharing Care of Your Newborn

That first week all my attention was on the baby, nothing else. Basically, both of us just tried to bond with her throughout that whole week. For me it was even more because I knew the next week I'd have to get back to work and to school.

When I went back to work, I felt bad. I got kind of jealous because I wanted to be there so much. They were constantly on my mind. I'd sneak in a call now and then just to check on the baby.

Mike

Your baby undoubtedly is a charming little person much of the time. Caring for him can be rewarding for you and for him. In fact, this can be a very special relationship for father and baby.

Having a tiny baby in the house, one who is awake and crying much of the night, makes it hard for either parent to get enough rest. Expecting mom to care for the baby by herself is not very rational. Caring for a baby takes a lot of energy. When mom and dad share the work, they are more likely to share the joys of parenting.

When I came home, I was really tired. About the second day I started to feel better. But my husband was there, and he helped me. He usually woke up at 3 a.m. for that feeding.

Zaria, 16 - Devyn, 3 months

If You Don't Live with Your Baby

Every time I don't work, about two mornings a week, I always have Julia.

I started taking her home about a week after she was born when her mother went back to school. Julia sleeps the first couple of hours, then I change her and feed her. I always hold her while I feed her. I'd never prop the bottle.

I've taken two classes on parenting, and they helped.

Philip, 17 - Julia, 2 months

You may have a close relationship with your baby's mother even if you're not living together. Perhaps you took prepared childbirth classes together. You may have been deeply involved coaching mother through labor and delivery. Perhaps you're caring for the baby as much as you can.

If baby's parents are not married, how much "should" father be included? If the young family lives together, they probably feel much the same about joint parenting as do married couples. If they don't live together, there is no pattern cut and ready for them to follow. Dad, however, can still play an important role in his baby's life.

Work out an arrangement so that your baby's mother also has some free time. Too often, the young mother is saddled with the entire responsibility of caring for the baby while the father doesn't even get to see his child. When this happens, everyone loses.

Sometimes the father feels left out because mom appears to know more about caring for their baby than he does.

Brooke acts as if I'm the babysitter, like I'm not his father. She finally lets me change him and feed him. At first she hovered over me like I didn't know what I was doing, and like she had raised so many kids. All she'd done was help people out, she hadn't raised them.

Joel, 19 - Blair, 3 months

Probably the best thing for Joel to do is become an expert himself. He's far more than the babysitter, and he knows it. He and Brooke need to talk through these feelings. Probably Brooke will become a little less nervous, and, therefore, less bossy as Blair gets a little older. One thing is sure — nobody would win if Joel decided to quit caring for his son because he thinks the mother isn't as positive as he'd like.

I'm going to do for Blair what I didn't get. My father wasn't always doing right. He wasn't around much. I took that into account, and I'm going to be a better father than I had.

Joel

Your child and you both win if you stay involved in his life. *Enjoy!*

*For more information, see **Teen Dads: Rights, Responsibilities and Joys** by Lindsay (Morning Glory).*

Sometimes Mom must parent alone.

7

Focus on Mom
and Extended Family

I would feel even more alone if the father had been with me throughout pregnancy, then left. But he left three months after I got pregnant. I'm not in touch with him at all. He's entirely out of the picture.

Sometimes I see a friend with her boyfriend and baby, and wish Orlando had a father. But other times I wonder if I'd want to share!

Holly, 17 - Orlando, 5 months

It makes it hard being the father and mother at the same time. It would help to have a father around, but there is nothing I can

do about it. When Pedro grows up, I don't know what
I'll tell him. His father never knew I was pregnant. I
put "unknown" on the birth certificate.

My big brother is around, and he holds him. I think
that will help.

Maria, 17 - Pedro, 2 months

About five out of six teenage mothers are not married
when they give birth. Some of these young mothers are
quite alone. The baby's father may have left when he
learned of the pregnancy. In some cases, he may not even
know about the baby.

Maria had a tough time for three years. She lived at
home, and managed to go to school fairly regularly. When
Pedro was three, Maria married Ralph (not Pedro's father).
They now have four children including Pedro.

The fact that your child's father is not around doesn't
mean your child will never have a father. A "real" father is
a dad who is actively parenting. Ralph is Pedro's real father
because he is the one who has taken that role.

Filing for Child Support

I want to get full custody of my daughter. I want to
make sure that he won't take her from me later on. I
feel very sad and disappointed because he says he
cares about my daughter. He says he wants to see her
all the time, but he has only been able to visit her
three times. We live only five blocks away from each
other, but he doesn't find the time to come see her.
His mom comes to see her all the time but he doesn't.

Lacey, 16 - Jenilee, 1 month

Lacey isn't sure she wants to file for child support. Some
young mothers choose not even to name the father of their
baby. They don't file for child support. "I can do it on my
own," they say.

This isn't fair to the child. Even if the father has no job and no money now, and you don't think you want your child to know him, it's still important that he not be shut out of his child's life forever.

If the baby's father is providing some financial support, and sometimes even if he's not, he has a right to see his baby. Legally, he may be able to have his child with him part of the time. If the young parents disagree on this matter, they should talk to a lawyer or legal aid group.

Both parents are required by law to support their child, whether or not they planned to have a child together. A child supported by only one parent is likely to be poor. As mentioned in chapter 6, he has a right to benefits from both parents, benefits such as Social Security, insurance benefits, inheritance rights, veteran's and other benefits. You need to establish paternity so that your child will be able to claim such benefits. In some states, paternity is established by both parents signing a legal paper saying he is the father.

If the father refuses to admit paternity, you may need to go to court. Blood tests are almost 100 percent accurate in identifying the father of a child. The blood tests are genetic tests which compare many different factors in your blood with similar parts of the man's and the child's blood.

Other People's Comments

Being alone during pregnancy and afterward is extremely difficult for many moms. Other people may make it even harder:

> *When you see someone with the father, you just want to cry because you aren't going to have a father for your baby. I'd hear all of these girls talking about the baby's father, and how we aren't together.*
> *They would ask me questions like "Are you with the*

baby's father? Are you going to get married?" You
have to answer them, and it's embarrassing. Some-
times you want to cry right then.

                                        Goldie, 17 - Jimmy, 3 months

You *don't* "have to answer them." It's okay to say, "I'd
rather not talk about it." You don't owe people an explana-
tion. On the other hand, sometimes it helps to talk about
our problems with someone we trust. When you're
parenting alone, having the support of a few close friends
can help a lot.

About half the children in the United States today will
spend at least part of their lives in a one-parent household.
Most people still think it's better for a child to have two
parents who care about each other. But a single parent can
certainly be a loving, "good" parent. It just takes a little
more effort.

Help from Grandma

My mom tells me little things — like she noticed
Isabel's bottom was getting a little red. She said I
should put a little Vaseline there. I did, and it went
away. The first time I made her bottle, I was crying
and didn't know how to do it. My mom said, "No, this
is how you do it." And she walked me through it.

                                        Mia, 18 - Isabel, 6 weeks

Very young parents, married as well as single, are more
likely to live with their parents than is an older parent. How
does this change their approach to baby care and child
rearing?

On the positive side, it is often reassuring as well as less
tiring to have some help with baby care. New parents may
suddenly feel they don't know how to take care of this

small creature. Having your mother in the same house can be comforting. During the early weeks of night feeding, she may even be willing to take an occasional turn at getting up with the baby while you sleep.

If baby's father isn't around, you may need more help from grandma. Many young mothers who live with their parents find the first couple of months with a baby somewhat of a "honeymoon" period. Your parents may be eager to help you.

> *I got frustrated one night. Isabel was hungry, but I wanted to change her first because she had pooped. She started screaming, and she got her foot in the poop, and I got upset. My mom said, "Can I help you?" She got the bottle for me, and said, "Calm down." That helped.*
>
> Mia

If you have brothers and sisters, they may fight over who gets to hold the baby next. Appreciate their help even as you do as much as possible for your baby.

> *My little sister and brother like to hold Tajanell. Occasionally they get mad and argue, "It's my turn to hold her." Sometimes they feed her, or they hold her while they're watching TV.*
>
> LaTasha, 16 - Tajanell, 6 weeks

"Who's My Mother?"

The neat thing about grandmas is that they're experienced. They've learned from their mistakes. They take time, and have learned how to be patient with a fussy baby.

The not-so-good news is that sometimes grandparents take on too much responsibility. They may appear to forget who the mom is.

If grandmother takes over in the beginning, it may be hard for baby's own mother to take charge later. The result in many families is a baby who thinks grandma is her mother. Baby's mother then feels left out and resentful. Most hurt may be the baby who isn't sure who mother really is.

I catch my mother occasionally playing the mother role. I can understand that because she has the experience. Besides, I really need that when I'm tired or don't feel good. But other times I don't like it.

I'll be playing with Karl, and she'll come in and pick him up and take him off with her. I don't like that at all.

Sometimes I have to explain to my mom that I have taken on this responsibility of being a mother, and I want to do it the whole way. I know when Karl is hungry, when he needs a bath, etc., but my mom still tries to tell me to do all these things. I try not to let it bother me — but it does.

                                    Kimberly, 17 - Karl, 2 months

Key — Taking Responsibility

I thought it would be my mom taking care of Racquelle all the time. With my two sisters who got pregnant at 16, she took over. They didn't know anything about taking care of their babies.

When I brought Racquelle home, I took care of her by myself all the time. I showed my mom I could do it. So now that she knows she doesn't have to take care of her, she will babysit sometimes when I want to go out.

                                    Cheryl, 15 - Racquelle, 2 months

Sometimes young mothers have more help than they

want. If this happens to you, perhaps you can help your family understand that all of you — your parents, siblings, baby, and you — will be better off if you take the primary responsibility for caring for your child. If you start out, tired as you are, showing them that you know how to be a good parent, they may be less likely to give you more help and advice than you feel you need.

If you're a young parent living with your parents, you may feel you have no choice. You probably also appreciate their help. An extended family of baby, mother, and/or father, and grandparents at its best means more love and TLC (Tender Loving Care) for baby — and that's great!

Living with Partner's Family

If you move in with your partner's family (whether you're the mother or father), there may be added difficulties. No two families are alike, and those differences may demand a lot of understanding on everybody's part.

At my house there were only four of us. There's lots of them here. Ten people live in this house, and there's lots of noise — loud TV, loud music. It bothers me, but I have to get used to it.

Allegra, 17 - Navaeh, 6 weeks

If you're from a different culture than your partner, it may be even harder.

It's real hard because Colin's family are all in a different culture. I'm white, and they're Mexican. That makes it hard. They have different upbringing than I have. I feel like I'm being forced to grow up the way they grew up, and I'm not used to that.

Are we going to bring Clancy up to know both English and Spanish, or just English? I would like him to know both languages, but hopefully I would teach

him to speak Spanish only to those in the family who
speak only Spanish. There are a lot of them.
*   I'm trying to learn Spanish, but I find it real hard*
to communicate with his family. When they want to
know about the baby I usually go through Colin or his
dad, who know both languages. I'm trying to learn it
so I can talk to Clancy in both languages.

                                    Chelsea, 19 - Clancy, 2 months

Chelsea is wise to learn Spanish, and to want their child to learn both languages. Communication is important, and that's extremely hard if you don't speak the same language.

Even if you speak the same language as your partner's family, you may have been reared with quite different beliefs and ways of doing things. Perhaps your father and mother share the housework and child care, but in your partner's family, mom does these things by herself.

Life is seldom easy when two families live together. If you're a guest of your partner's family, you'll want to do all you can to foster positive relationships. Your first task is to communicate with your partner.

Communication doesn't mean you tell him (or her) how bad his parents are. Rather, it's a matter of the two of you working together to work through the problems. Whether you're dealing with big issues or little day-to-day annoyances, do all you can to find solutions so everyone wins.

Everything is pretty good. Sometimes there are
hard times. We just talk it through, and once every-
thing is sorted out, we're fine. Not long after we
were married, his parents heard something at a
party. They were very upset. We sat together, talked
together, and cried together, and everything was
okay then.

                                    Zaria, 16 - Devyn, 3 months

Will Everyone Agree?

*My mom is really good, and she helps me a lot. But
on some things I disagree with her. I don't think you
can spoil a newborn baby, and I feel strongly about
that. I just don't feel you can spoil a newborn. She
needs all the loving she can get.*

*My mom tells me I shouldn't pick Patty up when
she cries, but I won't let her cry very long. I tell Mom
times change, she raised five, but I've learned some
things, too.*

Beth, 18 - Patty, 3 weeks

Whether you're with your family or your partner's, with
more people in the house, there will be more interacting.
There will be more people who may wake up when baby
cries. There will be more people who resent the mess of
wet diapers and other baby things around.

With more people, there will be more disagreement, too,
as to whether baby needs to be picked up when she cries, or
whether she is simply trying to get to sleep. "Don't pick her
up, you'll spoil her" can be fighting words if it's Grandma
talking to a young mother who is convinced that a
newborn's crying means something is wrong.

Your best defense is education. Learn how and why
things happen to baby. Your informed responses to
suggestions from others are great tools.

Three generations, baby, parents, and grandparents,
living in the same house or apartment means everyone must
give a little, sometimes a lot. When you get uptight, try to
remember that all that extra love can be a real advantage
for your baby.

Your baby brings big changes into your lives.

8

Baby and Parents — Changing Rapidly

- Other Caregivers

- Your Partner Relationship

- Another Baby? When?

- Lifestyle Changes

Racquelle is seven weeks old now. She looks more like a little girl, and she's a lot bigger than when she was born. At first I was holding her constantly. Now I lay a blanket down, and she's content to lie there.
Cheryl, 15 - Racquelle, 2 months

My lifestyle is entirely different. Before, I could just get up and leave and do things on instinct. But now we have to plan ahead and take about an hour getting ready to go.

You plan your life, too — she's with you so your life has to be different. Especially money — you can't just be spending your money on anything you want now.
Lola Jane, 16 - Bailey, 2 months

Other Caregivers

As you care for your baby, you'll see tremendous changes during her first weeks "on the outside." You're working hard and you may be exhausted, but watching her develop makes it all worthwhile.

Especially if you're breastfeeding, you may find it easier as well as more pleasant for both yourself and your baby if you don't try to take him out much or attempt to leave without him during those first weeks.

Soon, however, you'll want to go out, do things on your own occasionally. You may need to get a job and/or improve your job skills. If you haven't graduated, you need to get back to school. If you're lucky, you live in a school district with infant care on campus.

When you leave your baby with someone else, be sure to leave phone numbers for your doctor, a caring neighbor, the fire department, the police department, and exactly how to reach you while you're gone. Put the numbers where the sitter can find them easily. Some parents leave Medicaid stickers with a sitter if they're going to be gone long.

Whenever you leave your child with someone else, it's wise to give that person a signed medical emergency card. You could state, "_____ *has my permission to obtain emergency medical care as needed for my child."* Be sure you sign the card. Generally, medical care may not be given to a child without his/her parent's permission.

Your Partner Relationship

If you're with a partner, you may wonder about sex now that your baby is born. Guys sometimes wonder how long you have to wait, while moms are more worried about whether it will hurt, or if they even want to do it. Actually, you may be so tired those first weeks after delivery that sex doesn't even sound interesting.

It's important that you have a check-up before you begin to have intercourse after childbirth. The first time or two the tissue may still be tender, and each partner needs to be patient with the other. The vaginal opening will be about the same size it was before you ever had sex. At first, hormonal juices that help keep the area moist may not be working too well. Therefore, a lubricant such as KY jelly or the jellies sold for contraceptive purposes will help.

Another Baby? When?

Another baby? Not very soon. We're pretty careful with contraception because we don't want another baby right away. That would be hard because we'd be spending twice as much on diapers and everything else. It would make everything harder. It'll also be easier when Keegan is 3 or 4 because he'll know more. He won't cry as much. We've agreed to wait.

Randy, 17 - Keegan, 2 months

Couples need to think and talk about future family plans. How soon do you want another child? Many young mothers, married as well as single, don't want another baby right away. From a physical standpoint, their bodies need time to recuperate from the last pregnancy.

Breastfeeding won't keep you from getting pregnant. You conceive *before* a menstrual period. Even if you haven't had a period since you delivered, you can get pregnant. You could begin to ovulate as soon as two weeks after you deliver — which means you could get pregnant again. You'd probably rather concentrate on your baby now rather than starting another one right away.

Some doctors recommend the Depo-Provera contraceptive injection after delivery while you're still in the hospital. If you're breastfeeding, it's best to wait until your milk is well established — a week or two. If you choose this method of birth control, you'll need another injection every three months.

The contraceptive implant is also fine for breastfeeding mothers, while the birth control pill or the patch might decrease your milk supply.

See chapter 14, *Your Pregnancy and Newborn Journey,* for more information on family planning methods.

Babies often come by accident. If you don't want to get pregnant again soon, you and your partner need to discuss your prevention plan. You either need to abstain totally from sexual intercourse or you need to use contraception *every time.*

Lifestyle Changes

Often a teenage mother — and most fathers, for that matter — finds caring for a tiny baby changes her style of living a great deal. If you're breastfeeding, you're entirely responsible for feeding your baby. You may feel you're doing nothing much but feeding her those first few days.

I can't do the things I used to do like go to the beach. I have to stay home with the baby. I'm not as free as I used to be. I have to wash clothes and make formula. I don't get as many calls from my friends as I used to. That bothers me. I like to shop, and I can't go shopping as much. I'm not dating because I have to be with Chandra all the time.

Maria, 18 - Chandra, 6 weeks

As your baby matures, you'll be able to include her in some of your activities. Life may never again be quite as simple and carefree for you — no more deciding on the spur of the moment to take off for the beach or the river. Even shopping with a small child is complicated. But with extra planning, it can be done. Good luck!

Resources for Parents of Newborns

Karp, Harvey. *The Happiest Baby on the Block: The New Way to Calm Crying and Help Your Newborn Baby Sleep Longer.* 2003. 288 pp. $3.95. Bantam.
Offers techniques for calming crying infants.

Leach, Penelope. *Your Baby and Child from Birth to Age Five.* Revised, 1997. 560 pp. $20. Alfred A. Knopf, 400 Hahn Road, Westminster, MD 21157. 800/733-3000.
An absolutely beautiful book packed with information, many color photos and lovely drawings. Comprehensive, authoritative, and outstandingly sensitive guide to child care and development.

Lindsay, Jeanne Warren. *Do I Have a Daddy? A Story About a Single-Parent Child.* 2000. 48 pp. Paper, $7.95; hardcover, $14.95. Free study guide on request. Morning Glory Press, 6595 San Haroldo Way, Buena Park, CA 90620. 714/828-1998; 1-888/612-8254.
A beautiful full-color picture book for the child who has never met his/her father. A special sixteen-page section offers suggestions to single mothers.

_____. *Teen Dads: Rights, Responsibilities and Joys.* 2001. 224 pp. Paper, $12.95; hardcover, $18.95. Workbook, $2.50. *Teen Dads Comprehensive Curriculum Notebook*, $125. Morning Glory Press.
A how-to-parent book especially for teenage fathers. Offers help from conception to age 3 of the child. Many quotes and photos of teen fathers.

_____. *Your Baby's First Year.* 2004. *Challenge of Toddlers.* 2004.
224 pp. ea. Paper, $12.95; hardcover, $18.95. Workbook, $2.50.
Comprehensive Curriculum Notebook, $125 each. Morning Glory.
*How-to-parent books especially for teenage parents. Lots of quotes from
teenage parents who share their experiences with their children.*

_____, and Jean Brunelli. *Your Pregnancy and Newborn Journey.*
2004. 224 pp. Paper, $12.95; hardcover, $18.95. Workbook, $2.50.
Comprehensive Curriculum Notebook, $125. Morning Glory Press.
*Prenatal health book for pregnant teenagers. Includes a chapter on care of
the newborn and a chapter for fathers.*

_____ and Sally McCullough. *Discipline from Birth to Three.* 2004.
224 pp. Paper, $12.95; hardcover, $18.95. Workbook, $2.50.
Comprehensive Curriculum Notebook, $125. Morning Glory Press.
*Provides teenage parents with guidelines to help prevent discipline problems
with children and for dealing with problems when they occur.*

Renfrew, Mary, Chloe Fisher, and Suzanne Arms. *Bestfeeding: How to
Breastfeed Your Baby.* 1995. 296 pp. $14.95. Ten Speed Press.
*Marvelous description, with lots of photographs and drawings (150+) of the
importance of breastfeeding, and of how to make the process work.*

Reynolds, Marilyn. *Detour for Emmy.* 1993. 256 pp. Paper, $8.95.
Morning Glory Press.
*Award-winning novel about a 15-year-old mother. A gripping story, and a
favorite of teen moms. Also see Reynolds' **Too Soon for Jeff**, a novel about
a reluctant teen father, and **Baby Help**, another novel about teen parents.*

Wiggins, Pamela K. *"Why Should I Nurse My Baby?" and Other
Questions Mothers Ask About Breast Feeding.* 2001. 58 pp. $5.95,
with quantity discount. Noodle Soup, 4614 Prospect Avenue, #328,
Cleveland, OH 44103. 216/881-5151.
*Easy to read, yet thorough discussion of breastfeeding. Question and
answer format. Also ask about the **Babies First pamphlets,** same source.*

Williams, Kelly. *Single Mamahood: Advice and Wisdom for the
African American Single Mother.* 1998. 190 pp. $12. Carol
Publishing Group, 120 Enterprise Avenue, Secaucus, NJ 07094.
*Down-to-earth, sister-to-sister guide. Offers suggestions on how to deal
with work, school, child support, discipline, dating again, and more.*

Index

Ordering Information

To order additional copies of *Nurturing Your Newborn* ($7.95)
or to order other titles from Morning Glory Press, contact:
Morning Glory Press, 6595 San Haroldo Way, Buena Park, CA 90620
714/828-1998; 1/888-612-8254   Fax 714/828-2049; 1-888-327-4362
e-mail jwl@morningglorypress.com

Please visit our web page:
http://www.morningglorypress.com